Management of Value

London: TSO

Published by TSO (The Stationery Office) and available from:

Online
www.tsoshop.co.uk

Mail, Telephone, Fax & E-mail
TSO
PO Box 29, Norwich, NR3 1GN
Telephone orders/General enquiries: 0870 600 5522
Fax orders: 0870 600 5533
E-mail: customer.services@tso.co.uk
Textphone: 0870 240 3701

TSO@Blackwell and other Accredited Agents
Customers can also order publications from:
TSO Ireland
16 Arthur Street, Belfast BT1 4GD
Tel: 028 9023 8451 Fax: 028 9023 5401

First published 2010

ISBN 9780113312764

Printed in the United Kingdom for The Stationery Office

P002387256   c10   11/10

Contents

List of figures

List of tables

Foreword

When executing projects, whether as part of a wider programme or stand alone, the key objective is to ensure that the expected outputs are delivered in full and result in the realization of expected benefits. However, this cannot be allowed to occur at any cost. The resources needed to deliver the outputs must be used as wisely as possible. This statement holds for all types of project, whether developing a new facility, improving delivery of a particular service to its customers, or changing the way in which a part of an organization conducts its business. At the programme level, the overall strategic outcome needs to be delivered as effectively as possible within an acceptable timeframe. At the portfolio level, it is essential that an organization can express its priorities in terms of what will add most value to the organization, so that the programmes and projects can be aligned to deliver these priorities. These demands translate into having the ability to deliver value for money at all levels.

Management of Value (MoV™) gives universally applicable guidance to enhance and maximize value for organizations, taking account of, and reconciling, differing stakeholder priorities, their wants and their needs, organizational priorities, and the optimum use of resources. In short, it provides the means for delivering the best value for money possible, within the constraints of the environment within which the organization is operating.

MoV brings together a set of principles, processes and techniques to enhance and deliver best value for owners and end users alike. Ernest Shackleton once said 'Superhuman effort isn't worth a damn unless it achieves results.' With this in mind, it is important to understand the difference between wants and needs. We must be clear of the results we need as opposed to those we only want. We must ensure that we expend energy on the needful and not on the wish list. Only then will we truly derive the best value for the resources expended.

So where does true value lie? Only you can decide!

The guidance in this publication provides useful insights into these topics which we often take for granted, but which, when times are economically tight, become more important in ensuring people and their organizations operate at their efficient, effective and economic best.

This guidance is timely and I commend it to you.

David Pitchford

OGC Executive Director and Head of
PPM Profession in the Civil Service

Acknowledgements

The commissioners and publishers of this new Best Management Practice guidance would like to thank the following for all the time and effort they have contributed during its planning, development and completion.

Authoring

Michael Dallas (lead author)   Davis Langdon LLP and The APM Group

Stephanie Clackworthy   Analytika Ltd

Project governance

The guide was developed as a project under the management of a project board comprising:

Mike Acaster, OGC, project executive; Eddie Borup, BPUG, senior user; James Davies, The APM Group, project manager; Janine Eves, TSO, senior supplier; Richard Pharro, The APM Group, senior supplier.

Reference group

Proposals for the guide were presented by the authors to the following reference group for discussion and guidance:

Mike Acaster, OGC; Paul Chapman, Evolve Business Consultancy; James Davies, The APM Group; Paul Francis, Modus Services Ltd; Neil Glover, TSO; Michael Graham , UK Value Management;

Elwyn Jarrett, Symbiotic Projects Ltd; Stephen Jenner, Ministry of Justice; Gp Capt (retired) S. J. Kinder BE MSc BSc; Darren Ley, Maven Training; Matthew B. Locke, Lend Lease Design; David Purves, Marandale Management Training & Consultancy; David Stoughton, Value Kinetics Ltd; Peter Weaver, The Learning Habit.

Reviewers

We are very grateful for the time and consideration of the review group during the drafting of this edition and thank:

Andrew Ball, Audit Commission; Tim Banfield, National Audit Office; Claire Filby, Communications Consultant; Melanie Franklin, Maven Training; Michael Graham, UK Value Management; Sarah Harries, Openreach, a BT Group business; Elwyn Jarrett, Symbiotic Projects Ltd; Stephen Jenner, Ministry of Justice; Gp Capt (retired) S. J. Kinder MBE MSc BSc; Matthew B. Locke, Lend Lease Design; Sandy Mackay, BRE; Ronan J. Murphy, RPA; Dr Stephen Simister, Henley Business School; Victor Smart, Chartered Institute of Management Accountants; David Stoughton, Value Kinetics Ltd; Sue Taylor, APMG examiner; John Thorp, CMC, ISP, ITCP, The Thorp Network, Canada; Peter Weaver, The Learning Habit.

Introduction

1

1 Introduction

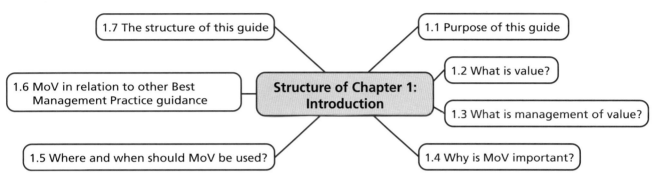

Figure 1.1 Structure of Chapter 1

1.1 PURPOSE OF THIS GUIDE

There has probably never been greater pressure on individuals and organizations, in both public and private sectors, to do more and more with less and less. For all organizations, finding the resources to meet essential and often escalating demands is putting unprecedented pressure on product and service quality and performance. There is a clear need to match what is delivered with the available resources, without undermining essential quality of the outputs, and to be able to demonstrate clearly that the decisions taken will maximize value.

Management of Value (MoV) has evolved from the tried and successful practice of value management across many sectors and over many years. This guide aligns the established methods with the Best Management Practice programme and project management guidance. The methods described in this guide are not new, but their use is often overlooked or misapplied.

This guide is intended to help organizations use a successful, proven methodology to supplement their current management practices, so that they can increase the value they deliver and make better use of resources.

Management of Value joins the Best Management Practice suite of guides aimed at improving performance for those involved in managing portfolios, programmes and projects in the public

and private sectors, known as the PPM[1] (Portfolio, Programme and Project Management) guides. It is equally relevant to improving operational efficiencies.

Throughout this guide, the terms programme and/ or project should be taken to include operations, whether stated explicitly or not.

The guide is structured around four integrated concepts:

- **Principles** – factors that underpin MoV
- **Processes and techniques** – methods and tools used in MoV application
- **Approach** – how to apply MoV portfolios, programmes and projects
- **Environment** – responding to external and internal influences.

In addition the guide contains information on how to embed the practice of MoV into an organization and four appendices covering document outlines, a toolbox of useful techniques, how to conduct a health check on MoV practice within an organization and finally how to assess and improve maturity of MoV practice.

These subjects are arranged over seven chapters and four appendices, as illustrated in Figure 1.6.

This introduction is intended to inform senior management who may be introducing MoV to portfolios, programmes, projects or operations, or who wish to enhance other management methods of delivering strategy.

---

1 PPM is the the accepted term in the industry and covers portfolio as well programme and project management issues.

There is also an *Executive Guide to Value Management*, a pocket-sized guide, which is published separately and intended specifically for senior management to help them optimize resources to enhance the delivery of essential benefits and thus improve value for money.

For the PPM community, this guide is aimed at those involved in directing, managing, supporting and delivering portfolios, programmes and projects. This includes senior management, programme managers, project managers, change managers and project and programme office staff and their sponsors. In addition, it would greatly benefit risk managers, to enable them to identify and manage opportunities effectively. It will build on the good practice provided in other PPM guides to maximize value.

MoV is relevant to portfolios, programmes and projects. In the context of MoV, portfolios reflect the organization's strategic objectives and set the agenda for the programmes that deliver the objectives, which, in turn, define the projects that deliver the required outcomes. At project level, MoV takes its direction from programme management, who set the agenda for delivering benefits for the organization. Outputs and lessons from the applications of MoV are reported back to portfolio or programme level as appropriate to inform management and to share lessons for improvement across the portfolio. Section 3.1.7 describes some specialist applications of MoV, particularly in relation to ICT and operational reviews.

MoV enhances the main purposes of PRINCE2™2 (successful delivery of justified business benefits through projects), *Managing Successful Programmes* (MSP™ – transformational change) and *Management of Risk* (M_o_R® – reducing uncertainty) with its main purpose of maximizing value.

It also shares with Lean3 (and to a lesser extent Six Sigma4) the principles of involving the customer, elimination of waste and greater efficiency. The main difference is that where Lean and Six Sigma aim to achieve efficient delivery, MoV focuses on **efficiency, effectiveness and economy**.

MoV helps to:

- Deliver more of the right things
- Reduce the cost of delivery
- Encourage more effective use of available resources.

When times are good, in order to remain competitive the demand is to deliver more for less. In leaner times, the demands are for cutting costs in a manner that inflicts as little harm as possible. In some circumstances, value may be added by stopping certain activities or projects. MoV provides a way of addressing this in an objective and auditable manner.

1.2 WHAT IS VALUE?

Value is subjective, with different people applying different criteria to assess whether they are getting good value. It is this subjectivity that makes it so essential to manage value deliberately, instead of leaving it as a by-product of any other management activity. In Figure 1.2, satisfaction of needs is reflected in the additional benefits resulting from effective use of MoV. The use of resources to deliver these benefits is shown in the bottom line of the equation. Added value is provided by the delivery of enhanced, but useful, benefits and more effective use of resources. Not all perceived benefits are actually necessary. MoV provides a means of distinguishing between needs and wants. Likewise the supply of resources is often (indeed usually) limited. Effective expenditure is essential to make the most of what is available.

Applied in the PPM environment, value is effectively a measure of value for money. This is represented in MoV as the ratio of satisfaction of needs (represented by monetary and non-monetary benefits, which bring the value) to use of resources (represented by expenditure in money, people, time, energy and materials – usually reflected in measurable cost). This is known as the value ratio.

---

2   PRINCE2 stands for PRojects IN Controlled Environments.

3   Lean focuses on the removal of waste from, say, a manufacturing process, so that goods flow to the customer at the rate determined by the customer, with minimal inventory taking up scarce storage space.

4   Six Sigma uses data and statistical analysis to measure and improve a company's operational performance by identifying and eliminating defects and achieving a high level of process capability.

$$\text{VALUE} \propto \frac{\textit{Satisfaction of needs (benefits)}}{\textit{Use of resources (expenditure)}} \\ \textit{(money, people, time, energy and materials)}$$

Figure 1.2 The value ratio. In the equation, the term 'needs' includes what is necessary and desired by the user

MoV recognizes that not all benefits are financial and that the differing priorities of key stakeholders need to be considered and reconciled. Expenditure must cover short- and long-term needs and recognize that resources are finite and must be conserved. Balancing and reconciling these conflicting demands, to maximize value, is one of the core principles of MoV.

Example

An international airport owner wished to increase its capacity by the addition of a new terminal. The national airline was keen to occupy the new terminal but believed that the facilities proposed by the owners would not maximize the efficiency of its operations. The airline's business case estimated an affordable budget of about $1 bn to upgrade the base facilities offered by the owner, but the airline had identified a programme of projects that would cost about $2 bn to achieve the operational efficiencies that it was seeking. It therefore undertook an extensive MoV programme to reconcile the difference.

The MoV team developed business cases for all the identified projects and then undertook a series of studies to justify their viability or otherwise. As a result of these activities the airline was able to select an affordable programme of projects to upgrade the owner's facilities. It also identified improvements to the efficiencies of its operating procedures. These combined to give the airline most of the performance improvement it was seeking and enabled it to occupy the terminal.

At the heart of these decisions was the ability of MoV to:

■ Determine which projects were really needed by the airline's business units by analysing their contributory functions, assessing the appetite of the stakeholders for the changes,

and calculating value for money, taking account of both monetary and non-monetary benefits.

■ Identify projects that could be removed from the scope that were not viable and/or represented individuals' wish lists and did not have the support of the business generally.

■ Halve the cost of the upgrade programme from $2 bn to $1 bn whilst still retaining the essential benefits arising from it.

1.3 WHAT IS MANAGEMENT OF VALUE?

MoV is all about maximizing value in line with the programme and project objectives and key stakeholder requirements. It is not simply about minimizing costs. The fundamental question that MoV is intended to address is 'Are we maximizing the value of our essential investments such that we are getting optimal benefits, at an affordable cost, with a known and acceptable level of risk?' Because value is subjective, MoV must also seek to achieve the optimum balance between all stakeholders' needs. MoV is a collective term embracing many processes that are aimed at maximizing value, which are explained or signposted within this guide.

A key differentiator between MoV and other methods is that **MoV focuses on function** – what things do to contribute to the outcome of an activity, rather than products or what things are. This functional approach can also be taken at the portfolio, programme, project or operational levels. Only when the functions are specified and outcomes are clearly defined in terms of the expected benefits does MoV explore different ways of doing these things to maximize value. **This approach enables MoV to improve benefits and (usually) to reduce expenditure and speed up delivery without impacting essential project scope or service quality.**

Essentially, MoV:

■ Enables more efficient delivery by employing fewer resources and using these resources to better effect

■ Provides a means to define objectives and scope clearly in terms of the organization's and end users' short- and long-term needs

■ Supports decision-making based upon maximizing value for money

- Encourages innovation that is well-aligned to the organization's goals
- Facilitates optimal balance between investment and long-term operating expenditure
- Provides a means of measuring and auditing value, taking account of monetary and non-monetary benefits and achieving optimal balance between them, thus demonstrating that optimum value has been achieved
- Enables effective consultation and engagement of stakeholders and end users and reconciles their differing needs
- Promotes sustainable decision-making, based on adding value, by addressing both monetary and non-monetary factors.

MoV enhances, rather than competes with, other management methods that also seek to achieve value. It is based on seven sound principles (outlined in section 1.7 and expanded in Chapter 2). These, if properly applied, identify ways to enhance performance and benefits whilst potentially reducing use of resources, rather than cutting costs at the expense of delivering much-needed benefits.

1.3.1 How does it do this?

MoV involves taking a team representing the key stakeholders in a project through a series of processes and techniques (called an MoV study) at predetermined points, usually coinciding with key decision points, throughout the lifecycle of the project. The overall process should be facilitated by an experienced, and preferably qualified, study leader. Most commonly a series of studies (each comprising a period of preparation, a workshop and activities to monitor progress in implementing the value-improving proposals arising from the workshop) will be arranged to inform each key decision point. In application to operational activities, the discrete study format may not be appropriate and a series of consultations will be conducted to take the contributors through the procedures.

The processes and techniques, which are described in Chapter 3 (Processes) and Chapter 4 (Techniques), should be conducted in a logical sequence. The purpose of these processes is covered in Chapter 5 and is summarized in section 1.7.2.

1.4 WHY IS MoV IMPORTANT?

1.4.1 Maximizing return on investment

Maximizing value does not happen by accident. Whilst intuitive approaches can be used to improve value, a formal process is much more effective, particularly in larger organizations. MoV provides a rigorous process and effective tools to enhance benefits and minimize use of resources. It provides an audit trail demonstrating how optimum value has been achieved. MoV is applicable to both private and public sectors. Private-sector corporations focus mainly on shareholder returns and the preservation of shareholder value. The public sector's role is to implement government policies cost-effectively and to achieve value for money for the taxpayer. MoV improves performance for both.

History demonstrates that investment in MoV is extremely cost-effective; the additional benefits are likely to be worth many times the total resources used in conducting MoV activities.

Examples

The US Army Corps of Engineers has been applying value engineering (VE – a technique from which MoV has developed) to construction projects since 1964. The savings resulting from this programme have resulted in the construction of additional facilities worth more than $5.5 billion without additional funding. Between 2004 and 2008 the agency saved $1.5 billion. The return on investment in VE studies has been more than 36:1.

The City of New York's Office of Management and Budget reviewed 101 projects of great complexity and diversity between 2001 and 2007. The resulting cost savings were $1.2 billion (4.7%) and the return on investment was $71 for every $1 spent on value management.

The California Department of Transportation, Caltrans, uses value management for highway construction, product studies and process studies. Cost savings are averaging more than $100 million per year; there have also been improvements in the quality of products, and greater efficiency in policies, procedures and business practices.

Source: Data from the US government agencies indicated.

For MoV to deliver its full potential, it is important to reward the correct behaviours in order to encourage people to make the extra effort. In the private sector, personal bonuses may be linked to some measure of company performance, which should be related to long- rather than short-term prosperity and returns. In the public sector it is just as important to encourage a culture that actively seeks to deliver value to the taxpayer. Setting inappropriate targets can work against delivering value.

For example, many contractors are paid a fixed return on capital investment in facilities to deliver services, without any requirement that such investment provides value for money. This encourages a belief that the more that is spent on something, the better it is.

Whilst additional spending might result in better services, there are too many examples where this has not been the case.

The disciplines introduced by MoV would reverse this practice.

It's important to note that simple compliance with MoV processes with no improved output is not a measure of added value. MoV cannot be successful in conjunction with the 'tick-box' mentality that a focus on process often brings. The only real measure lies in improved value added and/or performance, however this is defined, and not in the process itself.

Public- and private-sector incentives to maximize value should be carefully considered as a first step during implementation to ensure appropriateness. The subjectivity of value means that perceptions will change over time, so reward mechanisms must be regularly updated. The same consideration should be given to service contracts. This will ensure continuous emphasis on delivered value.

1.4.2 Customer satisfaction

MoV improves performance of products and services by addressing end user and key stakeholder requirements. It also provides a structured method of reconciling differences between the needs of customers or other stakeholders.

In the private sector, successful organizations have well-developed methods of monitoring and responding to their customers' needs and desires.

For the public sector, several national governments have published guidance on customer satisfaction measurement, for example in the UK, US and Sweden.

Although government focus tends to be on increasing efficiency in the delivery of public services, this needs to be balanced with the requirement to satisfy actual public needs.

> **Example**
> Peter Drucker, the well-known management guru, has been quoted as saying 'There is nothing worse than doing well that which should not be done at all.'

1.4.3 Risk management

In recent years, there has been an increased need and legal requirement for good corporate governance to enable the directors and officers of an organization to protect its assets, earnings capacity and reputation. As a result, there has been much emphasis on embedding effective risk management processes to avoid the destruction of value in organizations. Whilst risk management may identify opportunities to enhance value, it does not of itself seek ways to add value in the way that MoV does. Indeed, it can be argued that the absence of a constant search to maximize value exposes the organization to unnecessary risk, since it may not achieve its strategic goals. It is well known that it is necessary to take calculated risks to maximize value. The processes of risk management are complementary with MoV; each augments the other and together they provide a structured route for teams to arrive at optimum solutions and demonstrate good project and programme governance.

1.4.4 Maximizing people's contribution

It is frequently stated that people are an organization's greatest asset. They have the knowledge and skills to deliver the goods. Competitive advantage is commonly found in the tacit knowledge possessed by an organization's staff. However, the silo mentality that affects many organizations may work against capturing this knowledge. By deliberately engaging with a wide range of stakeholders and disciplines, MoV leverages this knowledge. It can, for example, unlock the talents of staff who are not normally consulted but can bring a quick mind with few preconceptions to difficult though well-defined tasks in a controlled and supportive environment. This promotes greater understanding of others' roles in the organization to give common focus, improved organizational learning and capacity for change. Most importantly, it encourages achievement of competitive advantage through facilitating and realizing latent creativity.

1.5 WHERE AND WHEN SHOULD MoV BE USED?

The processes described in this guide are applicable to almost any type of activity, including policy-making, programmes, projects, service reviews or product redesign. These include projects with visible and tangible outputs, such as those in construction, as well as softer projects such as organizing large public events or lobbying for support.

> **Example**
>
> An historic fishing village in south-east Asia was threatened with destruction due to the development of a new town. The residents turned to the processes of MoV to demonstrate that the long-term value of retaining the village (resulting from tourism and the preservation of the environment, both social and natural) exceeded that of replacing it with a modern housing estate. The case was so compelling that the authorities agreed to reprieve the village and even to invest in its refurbishment.

All programmes and projects are designed to bring about change so that an organization can respond better to its customers. MoV will supplement other activities to help deliver change efficiently and effectively.

IT projects are notorious for the perception that they deliver few benefits at huge cost and should be a prime target for MoV. IT projects can benefit significantly from the use of MoV.

> **Example**
>
> An asset management company needed to replace core systems supporting finance, HR and procurement. Within finance, MoV techniques documented necessary functions and used these to compile design specifications, providing a clear project brief. Once the new system was selected, the brief was used to communicate the scale of impending change to users and their customers in terms that related directly to how they carried out their work.

MoV has also been used to great effect to improve the delivery of local authority and other public services.

> **Example**
>
> MoV techniques were used to improve support services to children and refugees provided by two councils' social services departments. Demand was growing. An MoV study provided greater clarity of service objectives, helping to identify alternative, more cost-effective ways of meeting expectations. Both staff and management embraced the improvement recommendations enthusiastically.

MoV should be applied throughout the whole life of an investment decision, from start-up to retirement of any resulting assets or services. At all key decision points, formal studies should be undertaken. The focus of each study will evolve as the project develops. Retained records of such studies will ensure continuing recognition of:

- The rationale for each decision and the appropriateness of the proposals used to add value. Later decisions can then be made in the knowledge of which proposals were accepted previously, and earlier decisions can be revisited quickly if circumstances change.
- The expected benefits, which can be compared with benefits actually delivered as the project develops.
- The process followed, so that any weaknesses may be noted and improved in future studies within a project or across a programme.

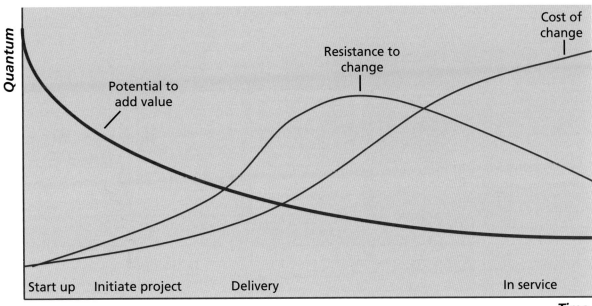

Figure 1.3 Timing

The greatest value from an MoV study will be added in the early stages of a project[5] because decisions taken and resources used as the project evolves represent constraints on making changes. Figure 1.3 shows that during the early stages of a project's life, when the costs of implementing changes to the project's scope are low, the potential for these changes is huge and the resistance of those involved to implementing beneficial changes may be low because people are open to new ideas. However, the ability to implement identified opportunities reduces with every decision made as the project progresses: the cost of making such changes increases because of sunk or committed costs, and resistance to further change may increase. The latter can be for two reasons. If the delivery team are contracted to a fixed price, they will not wish to expend effort on rework. Alternatively, after spending time developing a project, the contributors become wedded to their solutions and may perceive further changes as a threat to their professional judgement and reputation.

Example

IT products advance continuously and returns are maximized by delivering products in the shortest time possible. This is because customers want the latest technology and competitors copy the product. However, it may be advantageous to defer making decisions.

By using modified MoV principles – to allow design decisions to be taken at the last minute – it was possible to reduce development time on one project from three years to one.

1.6 MoV IN RELATION TO OTHER BEST MANAGEMENT PRACTICE GUIDANCE

MoV complements the suite of related PPM guidance developed by the Office of Government Commerce (OGC), which is aimed at helping organizations and individuals to use Best Management Practice to manage projects, programmes and services consistently and effectively (see Figure 1.4).

5   If Agile methods are used, there may be opportunities to defer decisions so that opportunities to add value increase during the design stages.

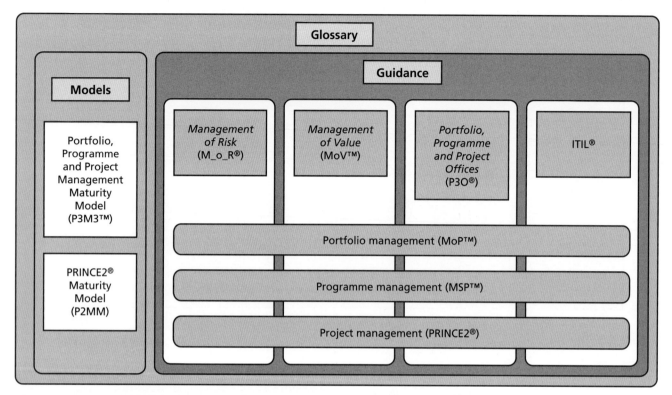

Figure 1.4 MoV's relationship with other Best Management Practice guides

In common with the other topics included in this suite, MoV should be embedded in the management methods used in achieving successful outcomes rather than regarded as an optional standalone or extra process.

MoV supports many of the core requirements of delivering successful programmes and projects as well as operational activities:

- Unambiguous definition of the intended outputs, aligned with an organization's strategic goals
- The functionality required of the project overall and its constituent products to meet the needs of the end users
- Addressing, quantifying and maximizing both monetary and non-monetary benefits
- Maintaining or enhancing quality and performance, including reliability and availability of the end products
- Providing clarity of the scope of programmes and projects
- Involving stakeholders and end users explicitly when describing the levels of quality and performance to be achieved
- Making most effective use of available resources expended in delivering the benefits
- Minimizing waste.

By addressing these topics MoV plays a key role in reducing uncertainty and informing management decisions based on value.

1.6.1 Management of Portfolios

Portfolio management concerns the twin issues of how to do the 'right' projects and programmes in the context of the organization's strategic objectives, and how to do them 'correctly' in terms of achieving delivery and benefits at a collective level. *Management of Portfolios* (MoP™) encompasses consideration of the principles upon which effective portfolio management is based; the key practices in the portfolio definition and delivery cycles, including examples of how they have been applied in real life; and guidance on how to implement portfolio management and sustain progress in a wide variety of organizations. MoV provides a means to articulate an organization's value priorities to inform decision-making. It also informs the development of strategy.

1.6.2 Managing Successful Programmes

Managing Successful Programmes (MSP) provides a framework to enable the achievement of high-quality change outcomes and benefits that fundamentally affect the way that organizations

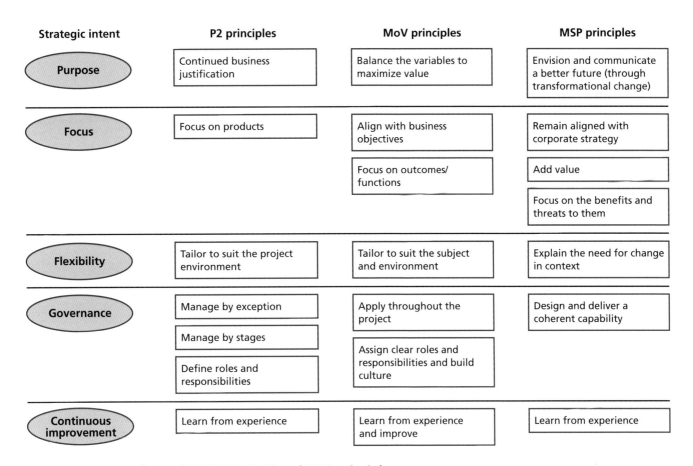

Strategic intent	P2 principles	MoV principles	MSP principles
Purpose	Continued business justification	Balance the variables to maximize value	Envision and communicate a better future (through transformational change)
Focus	Focus on products	Align with business objectives	Remain aligned with corporate strategy
		Focus on outcomes/ functions	Add value
			Focus on the benefits and threats to them
Flexibility	Tailor to suit the project environment	Tailor to suit the subject and environment	Explain the need for change in context
Governance	Manage by exception	Apply throughout the project	Design and deliver a coherent capability
	Manage by stages		
	Define roles and responsibilities	Assign clear roles and responsibilities and build culture	
Continuous improvement	Learn from experience	Learn from experience and improve	Learn from experience

Figure 1.5 Comparison of PRINCE2, MoV and MSP principles

work. One of the core themes in MSP is that a programme must add more value than that provided by the sum of its constituent project and major activities. MoV enhances the methods available under MSP to add value across all the constituent projects in the programme, so that higher performance is achieved.

1.6.3 Managing Successful Projects with PRINCE2

PRINCE2 is a structured method to help effective project management via clearly defined products. Key themes that feature throughout PRINCE2 are the need to deliver measurable benefits that are aligned to an organization's objectives and strategy, the management of costs, and quality. MoV offers proven methods of maximizing the benefits, maintaining or enhancing quality whilst minimizing unnecessary cost. MoV complements PRINCE2 in that while PRINCE2 focuses on the definition and delivery of products, MoV concentrates on the identification of functions and the required outcomes from programmes or projects and the generation of improved solutions, thereby justifying decisions about products and adding value.

1.6.4 ITIL® Service Management Practices

Where the operational environment includes technology, ITIL Service Management Practices provide internationally recognized guidance for IT service management through a very powerful base for understanding the business-as-usual processes and services to be improved. MoV gives guidance on improving value for money in the delivery of IT programmes and projects and also in the delivery of services that result from programmes involving IT, such that those services continue to contribute to creating and sustaining value.

1.6.5 Management of Risk

Management of Risk (M_o_R) offers an effective framework for taking informed decisions about the risks that affect performance objectives. Value and risk are two sides of the same coin and are highly complementary. By defining the needs and enabling their delivery in a risk-assessed, cost-effective manner, MoV increases certainty of achieving expected outcomes.

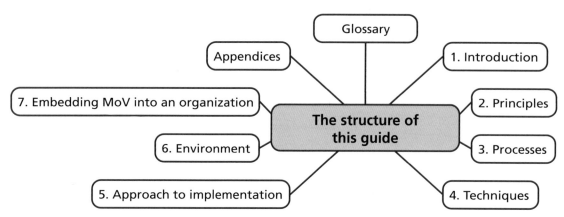

Figure 1.6 The structure of this guide

1.6.6 Portfolio, Programme and Project Offices

Portfolio, Programme and Project Offices (P3O®) provides universally applicable guidance, including principles, process and techniques to successfully establish, develop and maintain appropriate support structures that will facilitate delivery of programmes and projects within time, cost, quality and other organizational constraints. The P3O value matrix outlines how this support structure can provide resources, tools, techniques and skills for the assistance of project managers in delivery. These include the provision of skilled resources for MoV.

1.6.7 Relationship with PRINCE2 and MSP

The MoV principles complement in a number of areas those of other PPM methods, principally in their purpose and focus. They also have similar principles under the headings of continuous improvement, governance and flexibility.

Figure 1.5 gives a comparison of PRINCE2, MSP and MoV principles and illustrates how the methods can complement one another.

1.7 THE STRUCTURE OF THIS GUIDE

MoV is structured around six core headings, supported by four appendices and a glossary, as shown in Figure 1.6.

1.7.1 Principles (Chapter 2)

Seven principles have been derived from long-standing practice and experience and represent the factors most instrumental in delivering success. Whilst not intended to be applied in a prescriptive way, they are obligatory for good practice in MoV applications.

1 **Align with organizational objectives**
MoV applications are fully aligned with the organization's strategic objectives.

2 **Focus on functions and required outcomes**
MoV focuses on the functions that are necessary and sufficient in order to deliver the required programme and project outcomes and outputs in terms that clarify what value means for the organization, so providing the basis for making decisions that lead to maximum value.

3 **Balance the variables to maximize value**
MoV engages with all key stakeholders, reconciling their objectives to balance benefits and their delivery against the total use of resources, thereby maximizing value.

4 **Apply throughout the investment decision**
MoV is applied through all stages of the total lifecycle of the programme or project. Its focus will evolve as it moves from stage to stage.

5 **Tailor to suit the subject**
MoV is tailored to suit the project's environment, size, complexity, criticality and risk.

6 **Learn from experience and improve**
MoV applications encourage learning from experience and improvement by recording previous experience, creating an audit trail of decisions and actions, and sharing lessons across all projects.

7 **Assign clear roles and responsibilities and build a supportive culture**
MoV applications are supported by clearly defined roles and responsibilities. The organizational structure should engage the business, user and supplier stakeholder interests to build a supportive, value-adding culture.

1.7.2 Processes (Chapter 3)

MoV is delivered in programmes or projects through seven groups of processes that are described in more detail in Chapter 3. The seven main headings for MoV processes are as follows:

1 **Frame the programme or project** This examines how MoV informs the business case, supplementing existing information via specialist techniques.

2 **Gather information** Includes procuring information relating to the project, collecting the expectations from the MoV study, identifying suitable MoV team members, identifying and understanding stakeholders' needs and other project-related information.

3 **Analyse information** Analysing the gathered information to form useful input to the MoV study.

4 **Process information** Working with the MoV team to use the above input information to develop innovative and value-improving proposals.

5 **Evaluate and select** Selecting the proposals that have most potential for practical and beneficial implementation.

6 **Develop value-improving proposals** Working up the outline proposals into fully developed recommendations for presentation to decision-making management.

7 **Implement and share outputs** Developing the plan for implementing accepted value-improving proposals and monitoring progress. Gathering lessons learned and sharing with others in the organization for continuous improvement.

1.7.3 Techniques (Chapter 4)

A large number of techniques may be used with MoV. Chapter 4 seeks to describe only those that are used most widely. For ease of reference these are divided into two broad categories:

■ **MoV-specific techniques** Techniques that are either unique or core to MoV

■ **Techniques commonly used in MoV** Techniques that are most commonly used with MoV. Many other common techniques are signposted in Appendix B.

1.7.4 Approach to implementation (Chapter 5)

The MoV approach is defined as those activities requiring continuous and specific attention to ensure proper output from applied principles. They give clarity of governance and direction, underpinning MoV delivery, and comprise:

■ **Plan activities** If MoV is to be used to full effect, it is essential that activities are planned from the outset, rather than being added later, and that there are adequate resources to manage the activities effectively.

■ **Understand and articulate value** All organizations are different. The MoV team should understand what value means to the organization, be able to articulate it and tailor the application accordingly.

■ **Prioritize value** Some aspects of value will be more important than others. This hierarchy needs to be understood so that use of resources may be focused on where each will create most benefit.

■ **Improve value** Understanding and articulating an organization's priorities provides the key to identifying how value may be added.

■ **Quantify value** To express the expected improvements properly, it is necessary to quantify the value added. MoV does this for monetary and non-monetary benefits, as well as for use of resources, in the short and long term.

■ **Monitor improvements in value** It is essential that, once proposals for improving value have been identified and accepted, progress in implementing them and realizing the expected added value is monitored.

■ **Learn lessons** MoV includes processes for learning to improve individual and team performance, adding value to programmes and projects.

1.7.5 Environment: responding to external and internal influences (Chapter 6)

MoV must take into account the business environment within which it is applied. These considerations include:

■ **External factors**, including political, social, legal, environmental, technological and other parties' programmes and projects.

- **Internal factors**, including organizational policies, culture, other projects and other management processes in use within the organizations (including other PPM processes).
- **Programme considerations** relating to constraints imposed by the programme within which MoV is being applied and also by any external programmes which may impact on the application of MoV.
- **Project considerations** relating to the complexity of the project under review, other constraints within the project and external projects which may impact on the project under review.
- **Operational considerations** relating to internal or external operations which may impact on the application of MoV.

1.7.6 Embedding MoV into an organization (Chapter 7)

Many organizations will introduce MoV on a project-by-project basis, at least initially. When and if the volume of MoV activities justifies developing internal delivery capability, an appropriate management structure should be set up to embed MoV effectively. Chapter 7 describes a way to do this including:

- **Introducing an MoV policy** A statement setting out how MoV should be embedded and integrated with other processes so that it becomes part of business as usual.
- **Roles and responsibilities** Describes who should do what, whether full time or as part of other duties, and how these roles relate to other parts of the organization.
- **Setting up a plan for implementing the policy** Describes how the activities required by the policy will be implemented.
- **Introducing training** Explains how to ensure that the internal resource is competent to deliver MoV and that others in the organization understand and support it.

- **Study leader's handbook** An organization-specific document that describes how study leaders should apply MoV to programmes and projects.
- **Data capture and feedback** Explains how to capture information that enables the organization to learn and improve its MoV performance.
- **Monitoring and measuring the benefits** Discusses how to monitor progress.
- **Overcoming barriers to embedding MoV** Explores some of the barriers that may be encountered and suggests ways of overcoming them.

Example

A global consultancy embedded MoV in its organization using methods similar to those outlined in this chapter.

As a result, MoV principles have become second nature to many people in the firm and MoV processes influence business as usual. The organization has a large and effectively managed team of study leaders who can be deployed on all major programmes and projects in which it is engaged. The embedded culture of adding value in all its services has differentiated its performance across all sectors.

1.7.7 Appendices

A: Document checklists Suggested formats for commonly used documents.

B: Toolbox A guide to tools and techniques that can be used with MoV.

C: Health check Contains suggestions for conducting health checks to establish whether an organization is practising MoV effectively.

D: Maturity and competence Provides guidance on assessing an organization's maturity and individuals' competencies in the application of MoV.

Principles

2

Need to know what
we are doing

Produce 'Sound Bite' for Principles

2 Principles

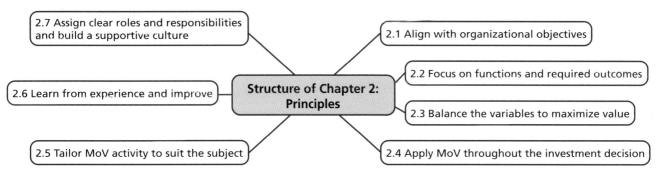

Figure 2.1 Structure of Chapter 2

This chapter explores the seven fundamental principles underpinning MoV:

- Align with organizational objectives
- Focus on functions and required outcomes
- Balance the variables to maximize value
- Apply throughout the investment decision
- Tailor to suit the subject
- Learn from experience and improve
- Assign clear roles and responsibilities and build a supportive culture.

For MoV to be effective, it is essential to apply the principles introduced above and described in more detail below. If these principles are not followed, MoV is not being properly used. The principles have evolved over the past fifty years through successful practice across many sectors of industry and commerce.

They are intended to provide clear and concise guidance to senior management and users alike. They are not intended to be prescriptive but to provide a clear framework for individuals and organizations to evolve their own policies, processes and plans to suit their particular needs.

2.1 ALIGN WITH ORGANIZATIONAL OBJECTIVES

Principle

MoV activities must be aligned with the organization's objectives or portfolio strategy to ensure a consistent and contributory approach across all programmes and projects.

The first principle of MoV is that organizational activities must all align with an organization's objectives. In the same way that every project within a programme is designed to contribute to achieving the objective of the programme, so every activity to maximize value must be similarly linked. Without such coordination, there is a risk that maximizing value within one project in isolation could diminish value across the wider programme.

Programmes are put together in order to fulfil the organization's objectives or portfolio strategy. Each project within the programme is designed to contribute directly or indirectly to achieving the programme outcomes. The objectives of each project should also be complementary to the other projects within the programme, ideally without overlap. Every product or element within each project should contribute to the project objectives. MoV activities must be aligned to maximizing value throughout this hierarchy.

Example

An organization was consolidating its activities from more than 50 sites, each with diverse operations and different standards of accommodation, to just five locations. One of the strategic objectives was to harmonize the way people worked across the whole business.

In a series of MoV activities covering the entire programme, a programme-level value profile was established. This allowed the team to align each project's value profile with that at programme level from the outset.

Using these, it was possible to ensure that the five consolidated operational centres were consistent, despite pressures from individual operators for different standards. Success was measured by the fact that all units adopted the same working methods and enjoyed consistent standards of accommodation.

2.2 FOCUS ON FUNCTIONS AND REQUIRED OUTCOMES

Principle
MoV focuses on what things do to contribute to the required outcomes before seeking to improve them. This approach clarifies expectations and stimulates innovation.

MoV focuses on defining what programmes and projects must achieve before seeking ways in which value may be delivered or enhanced. This ensures that the right questions are asked before leaping to preconceived solutions. For example, many buildings have been commissioned to increase available space or production, when what was really needed was a rationalization of current practice to make better use of what was already there or an innovative approach to obviate the need for the facility at all.

Example
A local authority was proposing to lease a nearby building in order to accommodate additional staff and facilities. An analysis of the functions performed by the various departments allowed the operational activities to be streamlined, reducing the need for additional staff and enabling them to share some facilities. The resultant rationalization obviated the need for additional space.

2.2.1 Functions
Functions describe what things must do, rather than what they are. Looking at functions provides the key to understanding programmes and projects and how they might be improved.

Functions do not simply apply to physical products but also to abstract concepts. For example, the function of a door handle may be to open a door; the function of a work of art may be to stimulate the senses; the function of a piece of software may be to enable an operator to work efficiently. Functions are normally expressed using an active verb and a measurable noun, sometimes qualified by an adjective or other descriptor.

At a different level the function of a programme is to deliver one or more strands of portfolio strategy. The function of a project is to deliver one or more requirements of a programme (assuming it is part of a programme, which is not always the case).

Functions may be arranged in a hierarchy to express their relationship to the programme or project objectives. Those that relate directly to the programme or project objectives are termed primary functions, whilst those that relate to other functions are classified as secondary, tertiary and so on.

The functional approach is central to articulating essential requirements in unambiguous terms that all those who are involved in the programme or project can understand. It is also one of the keys to stimulating innovation.

2.2.2 Value drivers
'Value driver' is another term for a primary function and expresses how to create value for the organization in line with its objectives. Even abstract requirements like 'proximity to public transport' may be expressed as functions such as 'enable easy access to public transport'. Value drivers are necessary since they are directly related to the programme or project objectives and, in aggregate, are sufficient to achieve the project's objectives in full. Value drivers differentiate one organization's or project's priorities from another's. They are used to judge the success of a project where they are delivered in full. They are one of the keys to measuring improvements in value.

Clarity in describing value drivers is crucial, since these will differentiate one project from another of a similar type.

Example
A budget hotel and a luxury hotel will have some common value drivers, but the descriptions of the primary and/or secondary value drivers will differentiate the quality and performance standards required. For example, some budget hotels will not serve meals, whilst luxury hotels invariably will.

2.2.3 Function diagrams

A function diagram provides a means of relating primary functions or value drivers to the overall programme or project objectives in a logical sequence by asking 'How?' and 'Why?' The diagram provides a simple method of defining essential programme or project requirements. There are two commonly used types of function diagram, the Functional Analysis Systems Technique (FAST) and the value tree, as indicated in Figure 2.2.

Abstraction is a term that indicates how far a function is removed from the products or elements that make up the completed project. Primary functions or value drivers represent the highest levels of abstraction. The products or elements represent the lowest. Asking the question 'Why?' increases the level of abstraction, while asking the question 'How?' lowers the level of abstraction.

2.2.4 Value profile

Whilst all value drivers are important and must be delivered in full to yield a successful outcome, some will be more critical than others to achieving the organization's success. This reflection of criticality is indicated by weighting the relative importance of each value driver. To provide a true reflection of the requirements for success, value drivers should be independent of each other. Assessment of weightings should also be tested for robustness against the risks of inaccuracies in estimation.

The weighted value tree is known as a value profile, since it articulates in clear terms the key functions that drive value and their relative importance.

The relative importance of different value drivers provides a good insight into priorities at organizational, programme and project levels.

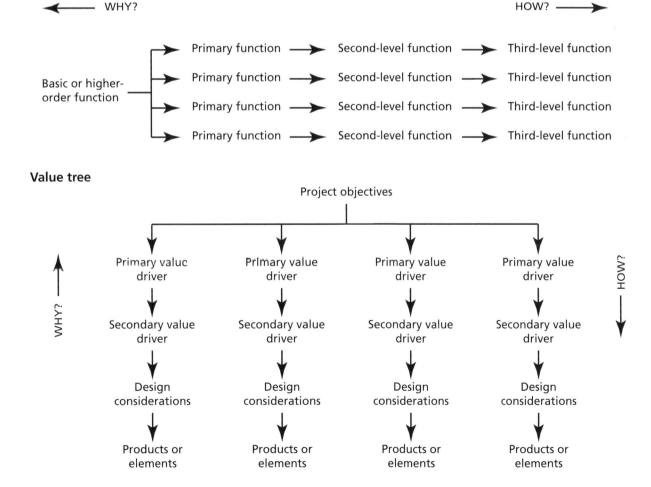

Figure 2.2 The principles of function diagrams

Example
'Ensure fastest delivery' might be the critical value driver for one logistics operation, because the speed of service might be the critical factor that differentiates that firm from its competition or perhaps the goods deteriorate rapidly in transit. Another organization may place greater emphasis on reliability and identify 'Ensure goods arrive in perfect condition' as its critical value driver.

2.3 BALANCE THE VARIABLES TO MAXIMIZE VALUE

Principle
MoV balances the variables to maximize value, taking account of and reconciling the views of all key stakeholders, the use of resources and the overall ratio of benefits to expenditure.

There are three main areas where it is necessary to strike a balance in order to maximize value. These are:

- Reconciling the needs and views of different stakeholders to maximize overall benefits by brokering a consensus on their differing expectations to deliver what they need.
- Balancing the use of resources to reflect their availability and the organization's priorities by redistributing across the different value drivers to reflect their relative importance.
- Balancing the overall benefits realized with the use of resources by optimizing the value for money ratio.

This balancing process is discussed in section 3.6.3 and is illustrated in the modified value ratio diagram in Figure 3.4.

Value is subjective and different stakeholders will have different expectations and priorities. These differences need to be reconciled to achieve a balanced outcome that achieves willing consensus between the different stakeholders. The value profile provides a means of achieving such consensus.

MoV is all about maximizing value in line with the programme and project objectives and the key stakeholder requirements. It is not simply about minimizing costs. Nor is it about delivering or even maximizing the benefits (at any cost). It is

a question of balancing the variables to maximize value. Value may sometimes be maximized by eliminating a service or cancelling a project.

The formal processes and techniques that should be used are described in Chapters 3 and 4. These should be conducted rigorously, regardless of project size, whilst the level of effort should be scaled as appropriate to the size and complexity of the challenge.

2.3.1 Engagement of stakeholders

Achieving the optimum balance described above requires that the views of all key stakeholders, both internally and externally, are taken into account and reconciled.

Stakeholders are those that can affect or be affected by (or perceive themselves to be affected by) the project or programme. They may be internal or external to the organization that is applying MoV or to the project to which MoV is being applied. Typically they may be end users or customers, the local community, relevant third-sector organizations, other government entities – anyone impacted by the study. The extent to which different stakeholders' views will be taken into account will depend upon their influence on achieving the required beneficial outcome of the project.

PRINCE2 groups stakeholders in a project under three main headings: business, user and suppliers. These include external stakeholders. Mindful of the environment within which a project is being undertaken, MoV emphasizes the need to encompass third parties who have an interest in the project (and those who may have influence over it). To achieve the optimum balances described in the previous section, it will be necessary to engage with all four groups of stakeholders and reconcile their different views on the variables (see Figure 2.3).

2.3.2 Reducing subjectivity

Value is subjective in that different people will place a higher value on some benefits than others. This particularly applies to those benefits that cannot be translated into cash terms, for example aesthetics or the ease with which management can take decisions. This subjectivity is particularly apparent when considering non-financial issues but is also present in issues with financial implications.

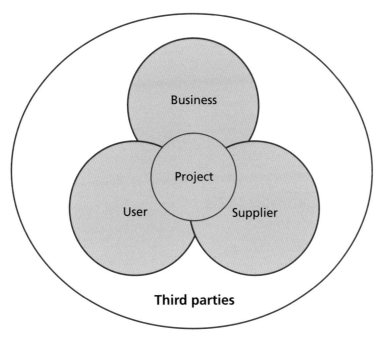

Figure 2.3 Programme or project stakeholders

Example

A railway company wanted to undertake a feasibility study for the re-invigoration of a substantial part of its network. MoV was used to test the appropriateness of the brief.

The end users were interested in performance issues such as reliability, maintainability and adaptability, whereas internal stakeholders were predominantly focused on the financial aspects of the business case.

The outcome of the study was a significant re-drafting of the feasibility study brief to include the end users' views. Success was demonstrated by the buy-in to the revised feasibility remit and the resolution by the company to conduct similar consultation exercises on all future major projects.

2.3.3 Balancing the use of resources

The value profile provides the key to trading off the use of different resources to optimize value. This includes all resources used in the delivery of the benefits, not only costs, and should include such items as time, people, materials and energy. Elapsed time in delivering a project is a resource. However, time can also be a value driver; for example, time to market may be a dominant value driver. In such cases, increased expenditure on materials

and people may reduce the time to market. Articulating such trade-offs and achieving the optimum balance are critical to maximizing value.

Examples

Time to market is critical in many fields.

For example, in the oil industry the sooner production can be brought on stream, the sooner revenue will start to flow. The additional revenue from early production is likely to far outweigh the additional costs of accelerating the installation of the production facility. Similarly, launching a new toy in time for Christmas is critical to its success.

2.3.4 Balancing benefits realized against use of resources

The greater the benefits delivered and the fewer resources that are used in doing so, the higher the value ratio. Whether benefits are increased or decreased, or whether the use of resources is increased or decreased, the challenge lies in achieving the optimum balance in the prevailing circumstances, i.e. the balance which leads to the highest value ratio. The ideal situation, of course, is where it is possible to increase benefits delivered and reduce resources used. By contrast, it is possible to increase value using increased resources, provided the increase in value is greater than the increase in resources.

Example

By spending more on training staff and improving the environment in a hospital, patients may recover more quickly and need to spend less time as inpatients. The benefits of improved capacity to treat patients may outweigh the additional cost of training and improving the environment.

There is also the additional benefit that patients will appreciate the speedier recovery and release.

2.4 APPLY MoV THROUGHOUT THE INVESTMENT DECISION

Principle

MoV should be planned and applied throughout all stages of a programme or project to reflect the evolving requirements in order to maximize value.

Throughout the lifecycle of an investment decision, the focus of effort under MoV evolves to reflect requirements of the stage reached. Those engaged in MoV activities should be selected because they have the skills and experience that are relevant at the current stage in the evolution of the project, thus enabling them to contribute effectively to MoV activities. In all programmes and projects, formal MoV studies should be undertaken at all key decision points to inform the decision-making process. The scale of the study should be matched to the issues to be addressed.

At project start up, information on which to base decisions is generally limited to that contained in the project brief and the outline business case. If the project is part of a wider programme, much of the information will derive from the programme vision and blueprint. When starting up a project, MoV clarifies the information that is available to assist in the development of a more comprehensive business case.

At later stages, MoV builds on the information generated to assist in making decisions; for example, the selection of options, based on value, informs the project and design briefs and provides a mechanism to enhance the benefits whilst reducing or making better use of resources.

MoV contributes to achieving positive reviews under the OGC Gateway Review process, for example by demonstrating that the project definition has been tested by the project team and clearly articulated at OGC Gateway 3, where the investment decision is taken.

Example

A critical constitutional project was allocated a red status at the OGC Gateway 2 Review. Application of MoV enabled the team to achieve a green status at a second review by addressing the weaknesses identified during the OGC Gateway Review. It also clarified the design brief. Subsequent MoV studies contributed to the project being delivered on time and to budget.

Once a project is completed, MoV can be used to improve operational performance.

Some programmes or projects, once completed, may lead to opportunities to improve operational performance. In other circumstances the programme or project itself may be about improving operations. In either case MoV may be used to increase operational efficiency, as well as its economy and effectiveness.

2.5 TAILOR MoV ACTIVITY TO SUIT THE SUBJECT

Principle

The scope and scale of MoV activity should be tailored to reflect the size, complexity and strategic importance of the programme or project.

From its inception in the 1940s to current practice, MoV has evolved from narrow, product-based applications to those informing the vision and objectives of programmes and projects in all sectors. In the same way, organizations should adapt and amend their MoV policies and practices to learn from experience and enhance effectiveness.

To avoid wasting resources, MoV should be adjusted to suit the scale and complexity of the subject project. Different projects will require different levels of MoV activity. At programme or project start up, it is advisable for the programme or project management to categorize projects in terms of their size, novelty, complexity and strategic importance. There is no point in taking a sledgehammer to crack a nut when a lighter touch will suffice. Likewise it is essential that care is taken to ensure the tools and techniques selected are appropriate for the circumstances.

A large and complex project may require that MoV is applied to different parts of the project throughout all project stages. A small and simple project will not require the same level of effort, and one or two formal studies throughout its life may suffice. Formal studies should be considered at all key decision points.

Where there are many small projects that are repeated time and time again, for example in the upgrading of a chain of shops, it may be worth spending more effort to maximize value on one project, since the benefits will be magnified by the number of projects.

> **Example**
>
> A retail company was embarking on a programme of refurbishment to refresh its brand. Several MoV studies were conducted on typical outlets to optimize the design. Although the effort expended would have been hard to justify against the small number of stores that were studied, the benefits of scale across hundreds of similar stores repaid the effort many times over, due to reduced implementation time and costs and enhanced sales.

Regardless of the scale of MoV activity, care must be taken to ensure the MoV principles are applied.

The level of MoV effort that is appropriate for the project and how it will be integrated with other project management activities should be ascertained by the project executive/manager and the MoV study leader at the outset, and a project MoV plan established. This should be incorporated within the overall end-to-end project schedule so that the whole project team knows when formal or informal MoV studies will take place and what their objectives will be.

2.6 LEARN FROM EXPERIENCE AND IMPROVE

> **Principle**
>
> MoV performance should be continually improved by learning from previous experience.

When embarking on introducing and embedding MoV into an organization, or using MoV on a standalone programme or project, it will take time to build up proficiency. However, benefits can still be achieved even with limited experience.

Undertaking MoV studies will help organizations to focus their scarce resources better on what matters to their customers, but will not necessarily improve proficiency in MoV across the organization.

It is one of the principles of MoV, in common with most management activities, that an organization should put in place a process for continuous learning from experience, using this to improve performance. Programme or project start up provides a critical time to take up lessons learned from previous experience, to avoid repetition of past mistakes and to build on things that delivered success.

Continuous learning should address three areas:

- Individual performance where individuals improve their ability to undertake MoV studies. This will come about through learning from their own experience, training, learning from other people's experience and increasing familiarity and confidence in applying the processes in different circumstances.
- Improvement in the quality of delivery of MoV processes. These should evolve by refining the MoV processes to match the requirements of the organization and the type of applications within it.
- Improving the organization's overall maturity in MoV.

Continuous improvement will be greatly assisted through the development and use of a lessons-learned database, allowing access to all involved in MoV.

2.6.1 Individual improvement

Improvement of individuals' MoV competence will be achieved through three main activities:

- Building upon their initial MoV training received to increase their knowledge of MoV processes and case studies.
- Gaining experience in undertaking their MoV roles and responsibilities (whether by managing MoV activities or process delivery).
- Seeking to improve their professional competence as indicated in Appendix D.

As individuals become more proficient, so they will be able to contribute directly to improving the evolution and application of MoV processes to the specific needs of the organization.

2.6.2 Process improvement

The MoV processes and techniques, described in Chapters 3 and 4, should be regarded as the starting point in customizing practice in an organization. Every organization has its own distinctive culture and way of doing things. The challenges faced by each organization and the applications of MoV will vary depending upon the organization's business.

2.6.3 Organizational maturity improvement

A realistic plan should be prepared to elevate the organization's MoV practices to the next level in the maturity model, if appropriate. Prior to implementing this plan, the benefits accruing from reaching the next level of maturity should be compared with the costs to be incurred by doing so. If progression is then recommended within a robust business case, it should be managed as a project in its own right, with clear objectives, resources and timeframe. The concept of improving maturity is explained in Appendix D.

2.7 ASSIGN CLEAR ROLES AND RESPONSIBILITIES AND BUILD A SUPPORTIVE CULTURE

Principle
MoV should be actively supported by senior management, clear roles and responsibilities, and a supportive culture throughout the organization.

Organizations that have sufficient demand for MoV to warrant building up their own internal delivery capability should ensure that there is adequate governance in place to support and deliver it. The process of introducing MoV to an organization and embedding it to the point that it becomes part of the way the organization does business is described in Chapter 7. It will be noted that it is not proposed that MoV requires a separate tier of management, rather that the roles and responsibilities of existing individuals relating to portfolio, programme and project management should be extended to include responsibilities for MoV.

Part of the role of the senior MoV practitioner, the person responsible for managing the MoV effort, will be to undertake activities and publish material to build a culture within the organization that understands and supports the concept of maximizing value both for the organization and the project stakeholders.

When applying MoV within the portfolio of programmes or projects, it is essential that individual roles and responsibilities are clearly defined to enable good communications with the teams involved at all levels.

Even if an organization is applying MoV on a project-by-project basis, it should ensure that MoV activity is actively supported and managed if the full benefits are to be realized.

Processes

3

3 Processes

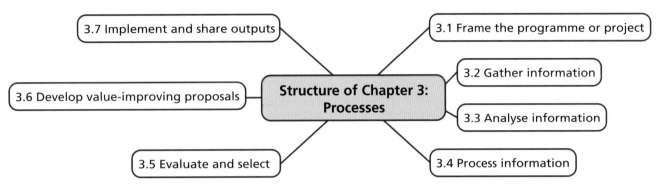

Figure 3.1 Structure of Chapter 3

This chapter describes the MoV processes that may be applied throughout the lifecycle of a project (see Figure 3.1). It also describes how MoV may be applied across a programme of projects, in IT and in non-project environments such as the delivery of services.

MoV activities change as a project evolves from inception, or start up, to use (business as usual) in line with the issues to be addressed, so that outputs at each stage support the project's progress. Some processes will be used at many stages, others only in specific stages.

The most common techniques that are suggested for use in the MoV processes are described in Chapter 4. Other techniques that are not specific to MoV are outlined in Appendix B.

3.1 FRAME THE PROGRAMME OR PROJECT

This describes how MoV can assist management to validate or challenge the need for a programme or project and define what is needed.

3.1.1 Initial briefing meeting

As soon as a project has been identified for the application of MoV, the senior MoV practitioner, or study leader if identified, should meet with key project stakeholders to establish the requirements for the MoV project plan (see section 3.1.5).

3.1.2 Informing the business case

The main objective of an MoV study at the outset, or start up, of a programme or potential project is to strengthen existing information so that senior management can make an informed decision as to whether or not to authorize initiation. This enables efficient development of a robust business case. An MoV study at this stage may be used to inform an OGC Gateway 0 or 1 Review.

The content of a business case is normally as follows:

- **A summary** The reasons for the project: a statement of the existing situation, or combination of situations, giving rise to the need for change. MoV can be used to challenge this statement and to find ways either to justify it or to re-state it such that alternative solutions can be found.

- **The expected benefits, dis-benefits, timescales and costs** These should be included in the statement of project objectives and should be given clearly and explicitly, focusing on the outcome to be achieved rather than proposed solutions. MoV will use the techniques for identifying and prioritizing value drivers, detailed in Chapter 4, to ensure that the objectives selected are those that reflect the requirements of the programme (if the project is part of a programme) or business needs, and that they have the potential to add most value.

- **The options** The case should explore several options (one being to do nothing) and recommend one for implementation. Options should be set out with estimates of their costs and benefits to demonstrate the rationale for the recommendation. MoV's emphasis on using value drivers as selection criteria will favour the option that adds most value in context, taking costs and benefits into account. At this stage the option not to undertake the project might be demonstrated to be the most advantageous.
- **The risks** The business case should include assessment of risks. By exploring alternatives and providing information to improve decision-making, MoV's value-improving proposals reduce uncertainty and avoid the potential destruction of value.
- **The investment appraisal** MoV can improve the viability of a project by maximizing the benefits whilst reducing the use of resources, including costs.
- **Procurement strategy** The method of procuring a project can make a significant difference to its value. The business case should explore several options and recommend a reasoned procurement strategy. MoV can be used to inform the selection of the preferred strategy.

3.1.3 Stakeholder analysis

Stakeholder analysis is a complex subject. In MoV, stakeholder mapping is used to ensure that the appropriate stakeholders are consulted or involved in the MoV processes. Stakeholders are grouped according to their degree of influence (or power), the interest they have in the project and whether they support it or not. This provides a means of prioritizing the stakeholders who need to be consulted in an MoV study.

Whilst all stakeholders should be involved as far as possible, it is reasonable to focus on building an active relationship with those who have the power to block or facilitate delivery. Stakeholders with less power but great interest can form strong allies; they can help to influence those who are more powerful and encourage others who are less interested not to become detractors.

Example

A group of councillors was vigorously opposing the relocation of a school to new premises. Analysis of the root causes behind their objections uncovered the fact that they were not opposed to the re-siting of the school so much as the fact that they lived next to the existing school and feared that the redevelopment of the site would devalue their homes.

Once this was understood, the negotiations focused on reassuring the councillors that the redevelopment would not have the impact that they feared, resulting in them withdrawing their objections.

3.1.4 Use of a value profile to inform programme and project objectives

An essential part of the business case is the statement of project objectives. There is no point in starting a project unless there is agreement on its purpose. MoV helps to identify the primary value drivers and relate them to the project objectives using a weighted value tree.

This technique, known as value profiling, provides a useful method of testing that the requirements of project sponsors and end users are aligned, thus verifying that this is the right project for the business.

Example

A hospital pharmacy was exploring a project to make significant cash savings from its budget. MoV helped the department to recognize that the pharmacy's function was not so much 'dispensing drugs' as 'managing medication'. This was relevant to the whole hospital, not only the pharmacy. Whereas the pharmacy cost around £2 m per year to run, it influenced broader hospital costs of around £19 m.

The resulting value-improving proposals included shorter average patient stay, less potential litigation and savings in nursing time. The cost savings amounted to one year's total cost of the pharmacy department for the hospital, far greater than had been expected from the original project proposal.

3.1.5 Developing the MoV project plan

The main purpose of the MoV project plan is to describe the purpose of a series of MoV studies to be undertaken throughout the project and how they will be implemented. It will identify suitable candidates to lead and participate in the studies, ensure sufficient training resource at the appropriate time and prepare specific management responses to value-improving proposals. With thorough preparation, the risk of delay in authorizing the implementation of these proposals should be minimized, thus ensuring that MoV is more sustainable within the organization.

The plan does not need to be a long document but should include:

- Introduction
- Outline of the issue to be studied
- Statement of business objectives (the intended outcome)
- Roles and responsibilities
- Specification of suitable candidates for the study team
- Training needs for qualifying candidates
- Specific management responses to team proposals, e.g. who will make a particular decision and how long this should take (this should include authorization levels)
- Process(es) to be followed, key decision points, deliverables and activities
- Nature and timing of the studies
- Tools and techniques to be used
- Reporting
- Quality reviews and controls
- Glossary of terms.

The use of the plan ensures that all participants understand the need for each study and what improvement is sought. The project sponsor may have specific demands that will shape the way in which the study is run.

3.1.6 Responding to changes in the business case

If the business case changes, for example in response to changes in market conditions, the MoV project plan must also change in order to ensure that the value profile reflects the changed needs of the business. This will have an impact on the selection of options or the development of value-improving proposals. It may be necessary, therefore, to repeat processes that have already been undertaken to reflect the changes.

Agile project management demands that the business case be revisited in the light of what is learned with each release of a product.

3.1.7 Specialist applications

In some circumstances the OGC Gateway model of controlling projects may not be appropriate, for example in some IT projects or the application of MoV to service delivery. In these circumstances some of the guidelines given in this document may not apply.

It is in the nature of IT projects that what stakeholders think they need changes as soon as they have an opportunity to use a working version of the product. Most projects allow for this by testing early models or prototypes before the design is fixed, but in some cases it is possible to continue to adjust the design until close to delivery. Many software and new product development projects incorporate this feature, which requires an iterative lifecycle and modified MoV techniques to take full advantage of the opportunities to maximize value.

This more flexible approach does not obviate the need to define clearly what stakeholders are trying to achieve – their value drivers. It does, however, require a willingness to adjust initial hypotheses in the light of new information, and it makes it imperative that goals are expressed in terms of desired outcomes and not outputs.

Properly executed, this process will reduce risk (because value-added solutions are facilitated through trial and error) and expense because many unnecessary features can be eliminated before development costs mount up. Repeated value analysis is used to select and prioritize potential features for development and the output of each iteration is reviewed in operation with end users to test their response to the changes and elicit fresh understanding of their needs.

Whilst project MoV studies are usually very clear on expected outcomes and who is responsible for their delivery, this is not always the case with service delivery studies. Since improvements in value will often be greatest outside the department originating the study, a great deal of stakeholder influence is needed to ensure benefits are fairly shared. Therefore, it is not unusual to involve additional stakeholders partway through the study as it becomes clear that they will be affected by a proposed service improvement.

Operational reviews may be conducted at organizational or operational levels and can vary significantly in scale according to their objectives. A public-sector cross-cutting policy can affect hundreds of staff (and, in turn, many thousand service users or customers) and may require several months of effort. On the other hand, internal studies may be quite small, be of much shorter duration and affect fewer people.

3.2 GATHER INFORMATION

As a first step during any MoV study, information must be gathered to compile the MoV study handbook. This is a short document for the benefit of all contributors, describing the key attributes of the proposed study. Some of the key processes are outlined here.

The MoV study handbook should be proportionate to the size of the study and the familiarity of participants with MoV. For a simple study with informed participants, the handbook may comprise a few sheets summarizing the planned activities. For a more complex study, it may need to be much more detailed and cover all the aspects contained in this chapter.

3.2.1 Briefing meeting

At the outset of a proposed study, at programme or project level, the study leader should convene and chair a briefing meeting focused purely on study issues. This comprises a meeting with the key project stakeholders, including the project senior responsible owner (SRO) or project executive, the end users, the project manager, and other key identified stakeholders, to establish study objectives, scope and other information needed to conduct the study. In some cases more than one meeting may be required to cover the complete agenda (see Appendix A) with all relevant parties and to select the MoV study team (see section 3.2.2).

The briefing meeting gives the study leader all that is necessary to gather and analyse the information required for development of an MoV study handbook, which acts as a briefing document for those in the study team. This should include roles and responsibilities for all contributors.

3.2.2 Team selection

Team members are generally selected for their skills, abilities and capacity for interacting successfully with other team members.

The MoV team members will be nominated by the project's management team, with input from some key stakeholders. Ideally, a team should be drawn up on the basis of team members' knowledge of the issues to be addressed and their characteristics and skills in providing a solution.

At the outset of introducing MoV in an organization, it may be difficult to choose the most suitable study leaders (several will be needed, depending on the number of concurrent MoV studies anticipated). Over time the better study leaders and contributors will be identified and a preferred pool accumulated. They should be appropriately recognized and rewarded.

Similar considerations apply when selecting teams for individual studies. Usually these are made up of those who are involved in the project, with little choice available. The study team should include key members from the project team to include all critical disciplines and, where appropriate, external advisers. It is good practice to consider involving experienced people who are not otherwise involved in the project to bring greater objectivity to the study proceedings. This could also be achieved by a peer review.

In constructing the MoV study team, all key disciplines included in the project delivery team should also be represented. This ensures that when the MoV study team refines designs and project execution plans, all views have been taken into account. The stakeholders, who may or may not be involved in the MoV study, also need to have confidence that their views will be adequately represented in the delivery process as well as being included in the development of the MoV study handbook. They should therefore be consulted as discussed at sections 3.1.3 and 3.2.3.

There is a substantial weight of literature on team dynamics and personality profiling, which can be useful for building high-performance teams, to which the reader is referred in Appendix B.

Operational or service delivery studies may involve large numbers of stakeholders. In these circumstances, because it can be impractical to gather all stakeholders together, MoV studies may comprise many consultations with small groups in preference to larger workshops.

MoV works best when all participants work collaboratively together. If the participants have not worked together before, it may be necessary to conduct team-building exercises. A team can be defined as 'a group working together to achieve a common goal'. Team-building, therefore, is aimed at helping these individuals do this more effectively. Team-building is the subject of many management books and articles, some of which are referred to in Appendix B.

Example

In a wide-ranging review of a local authority's children's services it became clear that traditional methods were not engaging the right people in the change process. By analysing the service functions from a customer perspective it became clear that the various service agencies could cooperate in a cross-cutting partnership to make significant improvements in children's services. The MoV processes brought together the elected councillors and a wide range of other stakeholders and ensured a shorter and sharper review process.

3.2.3 Consulting with stakeholders

Although the stakeholders in a project may sometimes be obvious, this is not always the case. Steps should therefore be taken to ensure that all the key stakeholders have been identified; techniques for doing this are described in MSP.

The study leader should consider engaging with the following groups, to a greater or lesser extent, in any MoV study:

- The sponsors/owners of the project
- Representatives of key customers or customer groups
- The organization(s) providing funds for the project
- The project team, including project manager, commercial managers, design disciplines and, if appropriate, contractors
- Specialist advisers and/or objective 'off-project' experts

- Staff and/or potential end users or typical representatives
- Representatives of the external community who may be affected by the project.

Not all aspects of a project will be of interest to all stakeholders. For example, the cost of a project or the way in which the completed project will be operated may be of little interest to the community where it is located. However, people in the area may well take a great interest in how it impacts on their day-to-day lives. If their views are not considered as the details of the project evolve, they may be in a position to disrupt its execution or operation. If their money has been used to fund the project (e.g. through taxes), they may perceive it as poor value unless their views are reflected.

All major stakeholders for the project need to be identified and engaged. They should be provided with timely, specific and clear information regarding proposals and their impacts throughout the development process. Regular feedback on progress is necessary to manage their expectations so that unrealistic objectives are avoided.

In the early stages of a project, it is vital to gain the support of senior management and influential external stakeholders to arrive at the optimal project brief and select the most appropriate options. Capturing, discussing, aligning and agreeing the main objectives are essential actions. Failure to identify and involve all major stakeholders during the identification of objectives stage may lead to overall project weakness or an outright failure to deliver.

Throughout, it will be necessary to understand and communicate effectively with external stakeholders who may be in a position to exert influence over the project. Techniques for engaging with stakeholders are available through many sources including MSP and PRINCE2 – for example, stakeholder profiles and stakeholder mapping. In particular, MSP has copious detail on stakeholder management, and MoV would use these processes in preference to creating its own. Every effort should be made to ensure that each MoV study includes the stakeholders that matter.

Example
The generation of the development strategy for a multi-billion-dollar new town development in the Middle East involved a large number of stakeholders from different organizations. The MoV study leaders interviewed people in small groups or individually to minimize the disruption to their daily work. After analysing their findings, they presented their proposals to a small group of key decision makers for agreement before finalizing their recommendations.

3.2.4 Research and precedent

It is good practice to start a project by examining how the same or similar issues have been treated previously. The information for such precedents will be captured in MoV reports and be entered into the lessons-learned database. Initially, before an organization has built up its own database, study leaders and participants will need to access published data and material on appropriate websites. Analysing how others have managed similar issues can save a lot of time. Benchmarking against similar projects can provide useful data for establishing the performance levels of the project under study, informing the setting of objectives and targets and focusing studies on areas of apparent underperformance.

3.2.5 Scoping

At the briefing meeting, it is important to establish whether the study is to address the whole project or only part of it. If only part, then which part or parts? The distinction between constraints (which may be challenged and are therefore within the scope of the MoV study) and givens (which are excluded from discussion) should also be identified clearly.

3.3 ANALYSE INFORMATION

3.3.1 Function analysis

Function analysis is a key component of MoV, one which differentiates it from other management methods, including PRINCE2 which focuses on product-based planning. Function analysis seeks to gain clarity of what a thing does, rather than what it is.

All products have one or more basic functions. For example, a hotel must accommodate residents; it must also receive visitors and enable guests to check out; it may feed residents, although some hotels do not provide dining facilities; it may facilitate exercise through gym facilities and encourage leisure activities such as golf. These latter functions are supporting functions that differentiate one hotel from another.

Function analysis opens the door to three fundamental changes in mindset:

- Until the purpose of something is defined, it is not possible to assign a value to it. For example, a brick has little or no value until it is put to use. As a door stop, its value is very low; as a part of a decorative façade, it may have considerable value.
- Understanding what things do provides greater insight into the overall purpose and required performance of elements within a project, leading to a better understanding of the project itself.
- Asking the question 'How else could we perform the function of this part of the project?' stimulates the generation of innovative alternatives that may perform better at less cost, rather than simply seeking different versions of the same part.

Function analysis is described in more detail in Chapter 4.

3.3.2 Resource analysis

To maximize value, it is essential that the MoV team has a good understanding of the resources used in delivering the benefits.

3.3.2.1 Cost estimation

There are many methods for estimating capital and whole-life costs, different methods being used in different sectors.

The construction industry uses methods such as the Building Cost Information Service (BCIS) under which total installed costs of an element are estimated against precedent and market trends. The estimates include allowances for waste, poor performance and risk. Care should therefore be taken to avoid 'double counting'. The estimates are usually market-tested to refine the expected out-turn costs of a project.

Engineering works often calculate costs of equipment and installation separately to arrive at total installed costs.

Operating and running costs are built up from known labour costs, estimated labour requirements and data from similar operations. Obtaining these costs can involve significant research. Estimating future cash flows relies on forecasting trends, which can be a very inexact science. The accuracy of cash flows using these estimates will have a significant impact on calculating whole-life costs or net present values and should always be treated with caution.

Commonly, an initial model is tabled and successively refined as more data becomes available. This applies particularly when calculating costs on IT and change projects, as these also suffer from uncertainties of scope. It is recommended that the study team agrees during the selection process what level of confidence is adequate to support a decision, so that the project can move on quickly.

There are several techniques for presenting the information that has been gathered in ways which will aid understanding of the key drivers of cost, time and use of materials.

3.3.2.2 Cost modelling

Presenting costs in graphical format (see Figure 3.2) can make it much easier for the non-expert to understand the causes of the major costs and their magnitude. There are a great many cost-modelling techniques, for which signposts may be found in Appendix B.

3.3.2.3 Time analysis

Most projects should have a logic-linked, end-to-end schedule (see Figure 3.3), typically prepared using computer software. This can be used to prepare simple graphical formats that clearly indicate the key milestones and decision points in a project. Sometimes a simple schedule of key dates is sufficient to enable team understanding.

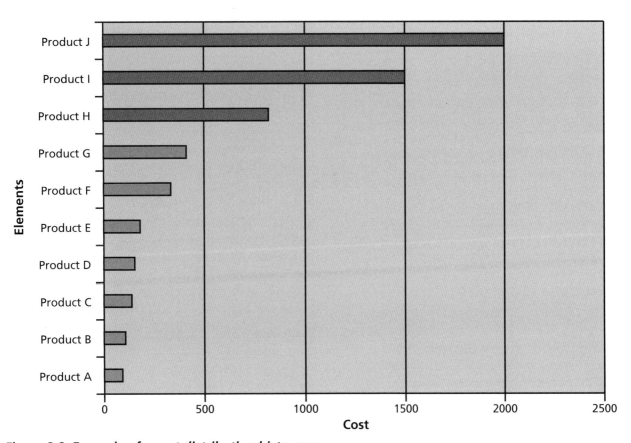

Figure 3.2 Example of a cost distribution histogram

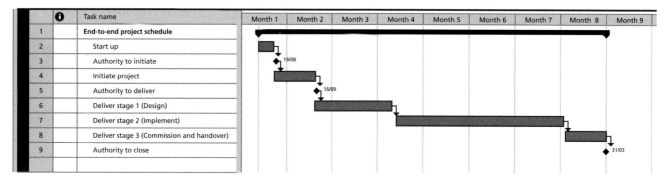

	ⓘ	Task name	Month 1	Month 2	Month 3	Month 4	Month 5	Month 6	Month 7	Month 8	Month 9
1		**End-to-end project schedule**									
2		Start up									
3		Authority to initiate	19/08								
4		Initiate project									
5		Authority to deliver		16/09							
6		Deliver stage 1 (Design)									
7		Deliver stage 2 (Implement)									
8		Deliver stage 3 (Commission and handover)									
9		Authority to close									31/03

Figure 3.3 Example of an end-to-end project schedule

3.3.2.4 Material analysis

Where a project involves the use of materials, the use of graphical images, such as material usage histograms, can provide insights into the potential pinch points in a schedule; similarly, statistics on waste can stimulate proposals for its reduction. The same technique may be used for avoiding overloading human resources.

> **Example**
>
> The main objective of an MoV study into a complex scientific research building was to determine the most effective building sequence to minimize the impact of construction traffic on surrounding roads. The MoV team used resource-linked schedules to prepare traffic histograms to help determine the optimum schedule.

Pareto's law (the 80:20 rule) can help teams to focus on the areas of the project in which there is the greatest potential to enhance value. If, for example, cost reduction is one of the study objectives, there is a greater likelihood that 80% savings will be found in areas of high cost (the top 20% of expenditure) than where costs are low.

3.3.3 Function cost analysis

The ability to estimate the costs of value drivers (or functions), in conjunction with their relative importance, enables the MoV team to assess whether a particular value driver or function represents good value for money. Whilst delivering value drivers or primary functions is essential to achieving the project objectives, this should not be done at any cost.

This process also enables the team to redistribute the use of resources (generally represented by costs) from one area of a project, which might represent poor value, to another where similar expenditure will deliver greater benefit, thus enhancing value overall.

> **Example**
>
> A proposed new food production facility was running over budget and did not incorporate several features required by its owners. The MoV team drew up a detailed function diagram, prioritized the value drivers and analysed the costs for delivering each function. By identifying opportunities for making significant cost reductions in the areas of low priority, enough money was saved to fund the incorporation of the missing features as well as bring the designs back within budget.

Generally, costs that are presented in activity-based cost format are easier to convert to function-based costs than those that relate to products.

3.3.4 Benchmark analysis

Comparing the analysis of information for one project against other similar projects can be very revealing and highlight areas where value improvements could be made. This process is known as benchmarking and can cover all aspects of performance and resource.

Whilst any external comparison will be very informative, benchmarking exclusively with same-type organizations can mask opportunities for innovation. Benchmarking against a wider pool of other industries whose only common feature lies in the type of process being compared can furnish some startling results.

Example

A public-transport firm benchmarked many aspects of its operation with other similar organizations to refine its operational efficiency and safety procedures. An MoV study proposed that it should compare certain aspects of its operation with different types of business, including a theme park and an aviation company. This novel approach led to some significant process changes, enabling headcount reduction whilst at the same time improving safety standards.

When conducting an MoV study to improve operational efficiency or service delivery, it is essential to understand existing performance levels to use as a baseline for measuring proposed improvements.

3.4 PROCESS INFORMATION

At the heart of an MoV study is the need to process the information that has been gathered and analysed, using the processes described above, to develop value-improving proposals. Invariably, the study leader will work closely with the MoV team members to do this.

The most common, efficient and effective way to process the information is by means of one or more structured workshops, facilitated by the study leader and attended by all the MoV team members.

Sometimes, convening a workshop is neither desirable nor practical. In such cases the study leader will consult with the MoV team members individually or in small groups to achieve results. In these cases it will be necessary to build consensus between the different parties to avoid disagreements later in the project.

Whichever method is used, controlling the activity requires all the skills described in selecting suitable study leaders, together with the knowledge acquired from this guide and elsewhere. This section provides guidance for exercising good control over the process.

3.4.1 Preparation

3.4.1.1 MoV study handbook

This document should be prepared by the study leader, based on information gained in the briefing meeting. It should be distributed to the MoV team before the workshop or consultation commences. It collates all the information gathered, with such analyses as have already been conducted, so that the study team can work from an informed base.

3.4.1.2 Invitation

To ensure that all participants know in advance the venue, timing, purpose and agenda for the workshop or consultation, the study leader should distribute an invitation to each participant in good time beforehand. A suitable outline is provided in Appendix A.

3.4.2 Facilitation

Effective leadership of an MoV study requires comprehensive and specific knowledge of MoV (contained in this guide) and facilitation skills. In common with many activities, particularly those requiring people skills, practice makes perfect. Novice facilitators should be provided with as many opportunities as possible to develop these skills. This may be accomplished by encouraging them to act as assistant study leaders initially to build up their confidence and to hone their sharpness.

As a facilitator, the study leader is someone with the skills to orchestrate a workshop or other meeting such that full contribution can be made by every member. The facilitator's focus is on the process, rather than the contributions themselves. Facilitation skills may be acquired through training and will include the following:

- Presentational skills and the ability to command a group of experienced and often senior professionals.
- The ability to conduct group processes, including being able to decide when it is best to use a group and when best to work individually.
- The ability to know the difference between a group and a team and to motivate a group to work as a team. Some time will need to be allocated to introductions and forming relationships where teams have not worked together before.
- A sound understanding of workshop dynamics, allowing team members to focus on their contributions. The study leader will state the purpose of the workshop, set the ground rules and keep the workshop on track. This may mean dealing with difficult people and conflict.

Study leaders need to develop intuition for events that require their intervention.

- Capturing information generated during a study. The study leader also needs to record the proceedings and gather information during the study. It is often helpful in workshops for the study leader to engage a scribe, so that all data can be recorded and managed in plain sight of the team. Alternatively, they can be assisted by a data recorder or a co-facilitator where the circumstances support it.

- Handling conflict. Conflict is not necessarily bad – indeed, it can be very constructive, as long as it is resolved effectively. Selecting team members from diverse backgrounds and disciplines heightens the chances of a high-quality solution, but inevitably it also increases the chances of disagreement. Conflict can often reveal problems of which the study leader and even the team were not aware. Turned to good effect, this can lead to a solution and enhance everyone's understanding of the issues. However, conflict handled badly can destroy teamwork and lead to disengagement.

- Understanding the causes of conflict. Conflicts may arise from scepticism about the process, the presence of difficult individuals, or hidden or competing agendas. The study leader needs to acknowledge that an issue exists and move the focus off those presenting it, so that it can be discussed impartially. Therefore:
  - Let individuals express their feelings, as this will make it easier to manage their emotions separately.
  - Define the problem and its impacts and then determine the underlying need. It isn't a question of determining who is right or wrong but of trying to reach a solution that works.
  - Focus on why people have such strong feelings and the points they have in common, no matter how small. This might be a way to bring two sides together.
  - As much as possible, encourage objectivity.
  - It may be necessary to consider what will happen if the conflict cannot be resolved. There are several models of conflict styles and how to manage them, which are signposted in Appendix B.

- Generating team ownership and buy-in. It is vital that all MoV team members are kept fully involved in the workshop and consultation so that they feel that they have had every opportunity to contribute and participate in the selection and development of proposals. This involvement should continue throughout the study, including the opportunity to present proposals to senior management. Personal ownership in the proposals will greatly enhance the chances of their acceptance and implementation.

3.4.2.1 Dealing with difficult people

The presence of difficult people can be a cause of conflict. It certainly undermines efficiency. Some points to consider are:

- Behaviours are sometimes driven by a desire to get the job done. This isn't necessarily bad, though the way it is expressed may need management.

- Understand the effects of this behaviour, good and bad, and the personalities that manifest as a result.

- Sometimes, the behaviour of another is what triggers adverse behaviour. Consider the effect your own actions may have.

- Whilst most people invited to participate in meetings or workshops are collaborative and constructive, there are those who can be difficult to control. The following are some of the more common examples encountered, together with suggested means of handling them:
  - Those who will not contribute even when you know they have plenty to offer – invite them to participate, without threatening them; play to their egos by flattering them.
  - Those who like to dominate the proceedings – limit time for discussions or deliberately invite others into the discussion.
  - The expert who uses jargon which no one else understands, or who gives too much detail – don't be afraid to ask what a particular piece of jargon means. Often others in the meeting won't know either or will have a different interpretation. Ask for a short summary of what was just said so that you can record it.
  - Those who insist that theirs is the only solution that will work – getting others to contribute credible alternatives and solutions

that have been successful elsewhere in similar circumstances, or working out a way to allow this person to leave with dignity are two ways to avoid stifling the innovation of others.

■ When a new process is introduced in an organization it will take time for people to understand and become proficient in its use. MoV is no exception, and this may be the reason for some initial resistance to its use. The problem may be resolved by being patient or providing some additional training or mentoring to those involved.

3.4.3 Creativity and innovation

Function analysis provides an opportunity to assess which functions offer the most scope for value-adding change, leading to great creativity.

Two key questions that may be asked at this stage are:

■ Why are we doing it and what are the alternatives?
■ How can it be done differently and/or better?

The former question may reveal that the function is unnecessary, leading to the elimination of a product or part of a process.

Consideration of alternative ways to perform a function provides greater scope for innovation than considering alternatives for a product. Frequently it can lead to the elimination of an element altogether.

> **Example**
> One of the primary functions of a door is to enable access. Access may also be enabled by providing a zig-zag entrance comprising two overlapping walls. This eliminates the need for a door, facilitates better access and reduces initial and maintenance costs.

There are many methods of generating ideas for solutions, and a selection is offered in Appendix B. These include brainstorming, which is probably the most commonly used technique for generating a large number of creative ideas. The study leader should visibly record every idea, regardless of its merits, for future consideration (see section 4.4.2.1).

In order to generate the largest number of creative ideas, the study leader should firmly disallow any attempt to discuss the merits or demerits of each idea during the creative session. Such discussion will inhibit the generation of ideas and waste time.

A good session may generate several hundred ideas and the greater the number of ideas, the greater the number of acceptable innovations.

In IT projects, development methods also need innovative approaches, particularly where iteration is desirable. Other methods, such as agile approaches, which can support completion of time-boxed iterative processes, have been developed in response to this requirement.

3.5 EVALUATE AND SELECT

Having generated a large number of ideas and suppressed their evaluation during the creative session above, it is necessary to allow people to exercise their judgement to select suggestions that have greatest potential to enhance value. There may also be a number of ways to progress the project that need assessment on their merits in order to select the most advantageous.

Under MoV, evaluation of proposed solutions is generally undertaken by assessing their performance against the value drivers. This ensures that selection is based on grounds that add most value to the project.

3.5.1 Idea selection

There are several techniques for selecting the most promising ideas from a large number generated during a creative session. Each involves the MoV team, not the study leader, in applying their judgement based on their technical and project knowledge.

Essentially, the ideas are assessed for how well they satisfy the functions as well as the study objectives. Assessment against the study objectives may be made using several relevant criteria, for example:

■ Reduces capital cost
■ Speeds up delivery
■ Enhances productivity.

Alternatively, the team may prefer to use criteria that are related to the implementation of the ideas, such as:

■ Acceptability
■ Relative ease of achievement
■ Cost of delivery
■ Scale of the improvement.

All assessments are recorded, as some might be useful to other projects, even if not for the one under study. The best ideas are assigned to an owner, called a proposal owner, for further development later during the workshop or by an agreed date. Where time is short, it is common for owners to develop ideas into value-improving proposals outside the workshop; this allows them to work individually or with colleagues (who may not have been present during the workshop) to refine their proposals.

If time permits, or when it would be difficult to reconvene the team, developing the value-improving proposals in the presence of the whole team can be very effective, as an energetic atmosphere develops, enhancing productivity. If the proposals are complex, it may still be necessary to validate the proposals developed during the workshop before they are submitted for consideration by senior project management.

Where the value-improving proposals are developed or validated outside the workshop, the group of specialists charged with developing the proposals will need a clear brief and timetable to report their findings.

3.5.2 Option selection

MoV studies may be used to select options at two levels:

- At project start up or project initiation, the business case requires presentation of several options as referred to in section 3.1.2 above.
- During the delivery stages (which include design), various options regarding how to deliver certain aspects of the project may be identified.

Techniques for selecting options in each of these cases are presented in Chapter 4.

Example

An engineering firm was bidding to develop an offshore oil and gas facility. The brief from the owner of the field was simple: 'Maximize the value of the recoverable assets.' The engineers had identified ten potential options for developing the field.

A subsequent MoV study tested the options against eight value drivers and concluded that option number seven would best fulfil the objective described in the brief. The team then went on to identify ways of improving the selected option in terms of reliability and performance, reduced installation costs and time, and innovative thinking in order to differentiate themselves from the average bidder.

3.5.3 Cost benefit analysis

In the same way as costs of delivering benefits may be estimated by analysing the use of resources, it is necessary to estimate the value of benefits that are delivered.

Whilst many benefits have direct financial impacts, many do not. MoV provides unique techniques for assessing the non-monetary benefits, such as value-profiling and assessing the value for money ratio. These are presented in Chapter 4.

These techniques complement conventional cost benefit analysis.

3.6 DEVELOP VALUE-IMPROVING PROPOSALS

A key output from an MoV study is the acceptance of value-improving proposals for implementation into the project under study.

The proposal owner (see section 3.5.1 above) works up a detailed proposal, with costs and gains tested for sensitivity. A proposal summary document outline is offered in Appendix A. The study leader will need to liaise with project management to ensure that sufficient resource is available and allocated to the task.

Where two or more proposals compete, it will be necessary to develop scenarios combining different options to identify the package that adds most value (see section 3.6.8). The proposal owners must also take note of other proposals being worked up that might lead to conflicting recommendations being presented to senior management.

The study leader should convene and chair a decision-building meeting at which proposal or scenario owners present their ideas to a panel of senior managers. The purpose of this meeting is to discuss the findings of each proposal and agree whether or not it should be implemented in whole or in part.

The decisions are recorded and form the basis of a proposal implementation plan. This plan provides the project managers with details of proposals, how and when they will be implemented and the expected value improvements (or benefits). This allows them to monitor and manage the implementation process.

3.6.1 Proposal development formats

It is good practice to have all proposals summarized in a standard form for consistency (rather than as random forms of presentation, which may be difficult to compare).

The checklist offered in Appendix A provides a useful summary that can be used when presenting proposals to the decision-making panel, since it contains a summary of all the key information that panel members need to make a decision.

3.6.2 Peer review

This can be an excellent method of gaining feedback on strengths and weaknesses of the subject under study, allowing for constructive challenge and recommended solutions to be made.

3.6.3 Balancing the benefits and use of resources

One of the principles of MoV, introduced in section 2.3, is the need to 'balance the variables to maximize value' (see Figure 3.4). This should be done whilst developing value-improving proposals and so is described in a little more detail here.

There are three main areas where it is necessary to strike a balance:

- Balancing the benefits and expenditure on resources used
- Balancing the benefits between stakeholders
- Balancing the use of resources.

3.6.3.1 Satisfaction of needs (benefits) vs use of resources (expenditure)

The first of these is the balance between satisfaction of needs (benefits) and resources used (expenditure), as illustrated by the value ratio in Figure 3.4. The greater the benefits delivered and the fewer resources that are used in doing so, the higher the value ratio. Whether benefits are increased or decreased, or whether the expenditure is increased or decreased, provides a challenge

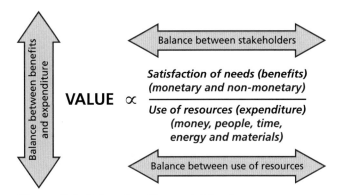

Figure 3.4 Balancing the variables to maximize value

to achieve the optimum balance in the prevailing circumstances, i.e. that which leads to the highest value ratio. For example if, by spending more on training, patients are cured quicker and need to spend less time in hospital, the benefit of improved capacity to treat patients may well outweigh the additional cost. There is also the additional benefit that patients will appreciate speedier recovery. The ideal situation, of course, is where it is possible to increase benefits delivered and reduce expenditure.

3.6.3.2 Satisfaction of needs

Second, value is subjective in that different people will place a higher value on some benefits than others. This particularly applies to those benefits that cannot be translated into cash terms, for example aesthetics. Many construction projects are likely to include a value driver such as 'communicate the brand' (referring to how the building will look). Tastes vary between individuals – one group of stakeholders may prefer one image whilst another will prefer something quite different. If both groups have an active interest in the project outputs, their views must be reconciled in the selected design to maximize value overall.

3.6.3.3 Use of resources

The third area of balance concerns the use of resources. The value profile provides the key to trading off the use of different resources to optimize value. These include all resources used in the delivery of the benefits, not only costs, and include such items as time. One organization or group of stakeholders, for example, may wish to spend more in order to reduce the time taken to deliver the benefits. Another may wish to reduce spending to a minimum since speed of delivery is not critical. Articulating such trade-offs and achieving the optimum balance are critical to maximizing value.

3.6.4 Value metrics

The value profile together with the use of scenarios provides a method of assessing improvements in value to the project overall, based upon monetary and non-monetary benefits. Quantifying value using value metrics is discussed in detail in section 4.1.2.5.

3.6.5 Cost estimation

When selecting value-improving proposals for implementation, it is not normally necessary to have completely accurate cost estimates for either the benefits or implementation costs to make a decision as to whether or not to implement. It is more important to achieve consensus between the study team members on the approximate costs for these items.

3.6.6 Assessing time impact

It can be difficult to estimate how long it will take to implement a proposal. A professional scheduler will have experience in estimating the duration and resource requirements of all the activities needed to implement a proposal and will be able to superimpose these, together with how they are linked and their dependencies, into the overall project schedule. Even if implementing a proposal takes some time, if it is not on the critical path it may not delay the project. Conversely, saving time on one proposal may not reduce the overall schedule because it may not be on the critical path. The schedule should include time for project management, for other discipline processes, for human elements such as holidays and sickness, as well as an approximation of the potential costs of any delay, whether incurred through interest, opportunity cost or value forgone. These extra factors may significantly increase the original estimate.

3.6.7 Assessing performance impact

Performance may be assessed by many methods, including monitoring benefits realized, throughput or outputs per employee, achievement of key performance indicators or financial results. Technical subjects may require assessments of improved reliability, operational costs and

impact on the natural environment. Performance improvements may also be assessed using the MoV techniques of value profiling and value metrics referred to earlier in this section.

3.6.8 Scenario building

Several value-improving proposals may be gathered into one or more scenarios, allowing the team to present a comprehensive package of activities that will provide the greatest improvement in value.

3.6.9 Specialist applications

In evolutionary iterative IT projects, MoV continues during development and becomes an integral part of each cycle. The prioritization and selection process begins when the products of each iteration are tested on customers and stakeholders so that progress towards targets can be evaluated and priorities adjusted.

3.7 IMPLEMENT AND SHARE OUTPUTS

The agreed proposal implementation plan should be filed together with the MoV study report for later comparison with results delivered. The plan will provide useful information in the lessons-learned database.

3.7.1 Developing the proposal implementation plan

A single MoV study is capable of generating a number of robust proposals. As part of the presentation of the proposals to the decision makers, an implementation plan should be drawn up.

A proposal implementation plan can be short – simply a statement of which measures are to be monitored and the scale of the benefit expected over a defined period of time. In many cases it will be an extension of the summary of all the proposals being put forward for discussion.

The plan should include:

- A list of the recommended value-improving proposals and the proposal owners for each
- A short description of how they will be included into the project
- The timescale for their inclusion, giving the scale of benefits expected over time

- Dates and method for monitoring and reporting progress
- A mechanism for review should progress fall below expectations.

Once authority to proceed with implementing all or some of the proposals has been achieved, the plan should be amended to reflect any agreed changes.

Winning commitment to change from those affected will be critical, especially if the proposal involves potentially controversial changes such as a reduction in budget or head count.

3.7.2 Incentivizing delivery of value

Unless there is a desire amongst those involved in MoV to improve value, it is unlikely to deliver its full potential. Staff may be motivated by MoV making the value they have added visible to them and/or linking this to rewards. Rewards need not be monetary but can be related to building pride in success.

> **Example**
>
> On an affordable housing project in Scotland, an innovation that was introduced following an MoV study was the 'save a tenner scheme'. Under this scheme workers were encouraged to identify ways to save £10 in costs per week by rewarding them with £10 per week for between 1 and 4 weeks. They could take the reward in any way they chose – the most cost-effective for them being to leave work early on a Friday, having completed their tasks, and be paid in full. The scheme proved very popular and resulted in significant savings for the employer as well as an incentivized and happy workforce.

3.7.3 Monitoring progress

The expected benefits resulting from the implementation of a proposal will be stated in the implementation plan.

Wherever possible, the measures for adding value should be the same as those that are already being used in the project.

Some projects may employ a process known as benefits management. This is described in detail in the MSP guide and provides a rigorous process for identifying, modelling, mapping and monitoring the delivery of the benefits expected from a programme or project. It does not, however, provide a ready means of maximizing benefits.

If such a process is being effectively employed, it may be appropriate to feed the value-improving proposals arising from MoV studies into the process.

The benefits map under the above process relates 'strategic objectives' and 'project outputs' in a similar way to the value profile. There may, therefore, be a way to integrate the two processes using the value profile.

If such a process is not being actively used, the realization of the additional benefits identified under the MoV process should be monitored either by the study leaders involved or by the project management team. The normal way to do this is to include an MoV progress report in the regular project reports, setting out the current status of the benefits realized.

3.7.3.1 Earned value analysis

Earned value analysis (EVA) is a project control tool that can be useful in monitoring progress. Essentially, it provides a method of monitoring costs incurred against progress and comparing these with what was planned. If costs incurred exceed those that were predicted at the time of review, it indicates that the budget may be exceeded.

3.7.4 Reporting

The study leader must prepare a report after every study to provide a record of the study and set out the proposal implementation plan.

3.7.4.1 Study output reports

Each MoV study will conclude with a separate report, describing the context and purpose of the study, the selected processes, the outputs and/or recommendations. Suitable document checklists are given in Appendix A. It is good practice to divide reports into two sections. The first provides a summary of the outputs, for the benefit of senior management. The second contains all the details needed for the project team to implement the proposals. The detailed reports will be made to the project director/manager and a summary sent to the senior MoV practitioner and/or sponsor.

It is common practice to issue reports in draft initially and finalize them after receipt of comments from the MoV team and the project manager. The finalized reports, including the implementation plans, should be disseminated to the project team to enable implementation of the recommendations.

3.7.4.2 MoV progress reports

Summary progress reports showing implementation progress should be included in the regular project management reports, so that the delivery of the benefits may be monitored and, if necessary, action taken to overcome any difficulties.

A summary of these progress reports should be made by the senior MoV practitioner to the sponsor and possibly to other senior management to inform them of progress in implementing MoV on programmes and projects. These reports may contain recommendations based on the outputs from the activities described above for refining MoV in the organization and are key to getting continued buy-in to the MoV programme.

MoV progress reports at project or programme level form a key input to embedding MoV in the organization.

Techniques

4

4 Techniques

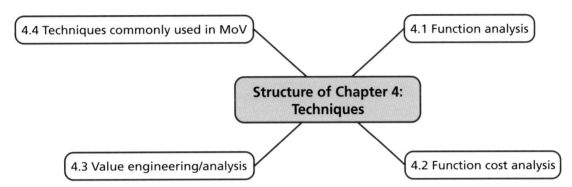

Figure 4.1 Structure of Chapter 4

This chapter describes the techniques supporting MoV processes and has been split in two parts:

- MoV-specific techniques, forming the first three sections
- Those techniques that are commonly used in MoV but also used elsewhere, forming the remainder of the chapter.

4.1 FUNCTION ANALYSIS

Function analysis is a key technique in MoV and underpins its second principle – analysing what things do rather than what they are and avoiding looking at ideas until functions are visibly mapped. As used in MoV, function analysis is very closely focused on customer needs and wants.

A function consists of an active verb and a measurable noun. A qualifying adjective or phrase, including a performance metric if possible, may be used if this adds clarity (for example 'Implement system', 'Implement computerized system' and 'Implement web-based system' are significantly different, spanning a considerable range of complexity), but generally the simpler the statement, the better it will be for generating alternatives. The introduction of the qualifying adjective or phrase is, however, critical when using function analysis to define a project and the expected levels of quality and performance (for example, 'Implement grade A computerized system' where grade A provides specification of performance characteristics).

There are several methods of function analysis. The objectives of the analysis are:

1 To gain clarity of understanding of the project aims and to identify what needs to be done in order to achieve those aims

2 To stimulate creativity in the search for different ways to perform the identified functions.

The fundamental logic underlying all function analysis is to ask 'Why (do we want to do this)?' to move from lower-order functions to higher-order functions and to ask 'How (do we propose to do it)?' to move in the opposite direction.

There are two main methods of function analysis: Function Analysis Systems Technique (FAST) and value trees.

4.1.1 Function Analysis Systems Technique (FAST)

FAST is a diagrammatic representation of functions and their hierarchy. FAST works by asking how the functions relate to each other. There are three main forms of FAST diagram:

- Traditional: designed to describe what the component parts of the study subject must do. It can be applied at any level.
- Technical: similar to traditional FAST, but, in addition, seeks to capture a time-based relationship, and functions that happen all the time sit separately from the critical path functions. It is generally used at subsystem or component levels.

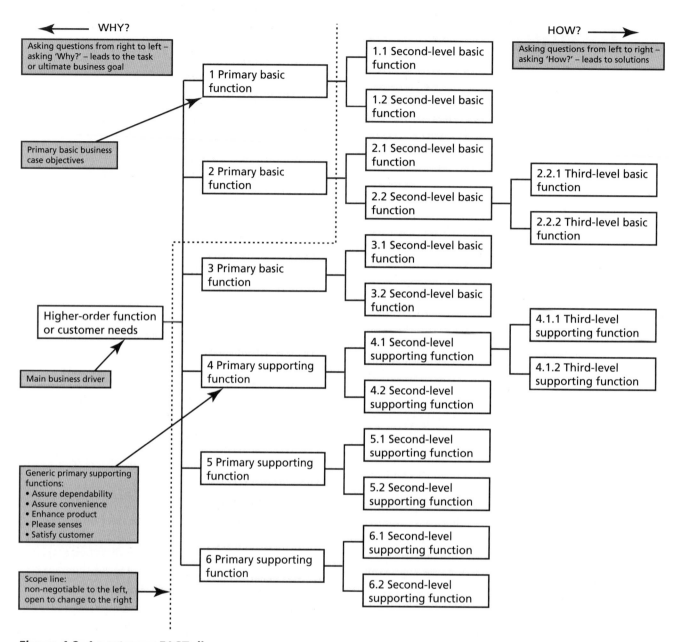

Figure 4.2 A customer FAST diagram

■ Customer: focuses on customer requirements or needs. Functions describe what the customer expects to get, rather than exactly what the product or service does.

Figure 4.2 shows a generic customer FAST diagram. The business or project objective (or customer need) is on the left and the primary functions stem from it by asking the question 'How (do we do this)?' The organizational objective for a product never changes unless the business case changes in response to a change in policy. This would also apply to each project within a programme, which would relate to the organizational objective for that programme.

The project objective or customer need may also be known as the higher-order function of the project. Each of the primary functions contributes to fulfilling the higher-order function. Primary basic functions are essential to the existence of a product. Primary support functions are those that differentiate one product from another similar one.

Generic supporting functions may be categorized under five headings: assure dependability; assure convenience; enhance product; please senses; satisfy customer. These are grouped together if all have been identified as necessary and sufficient to achieve the project objectives in full. Repeatedly asking the question 'How?'

generates secondary, tertiary and further lower-order functions. Reading the diagram from left to right shows how the primary functions will be delivered. The diagram stops at the right-hand side when the next answer 'How' would not be a function but a technical solution or product.

As read from right to left, it shows why the lower-order functions are needed. As a result, changing a higher-order function will lead to change in lower-order functions, as the reasons for the functions have changed.

Functions on the left-hand side (closest to the project objectives or higher-order function) are said to have the highest levels of abstraction (see also section 2.2.3). Moving towards the right-hand side of the diagram, the functions have a lower level of abstraction. The lowest level of abstraction is a tangible solution or product. The higher the level of abstraction, the greater is the potential for adding value.

A complex project may give rise to a great number of functions to examine for inclusion in the diagram. To do this thoroughly, FAST diagrams need significant effort and time to develop. You cannot do them quickly!

It is often the case when developing a FAST diagram that lower-order functions are confused with solutions to delivering the higher-order functions. This is not desirable, as potential solutions are generated later in the process (see section 4.4) so these entries are excluded from the diagram. The primary functions are normally arranged in priority order, with the more important nearer the top of the chart.

Classic FAST and technical FAST are seldom used for project MoV. They are very precise and provide an excellent way to describe the functions in a product or a process. It can be a rather laborious method of describing a whole project.

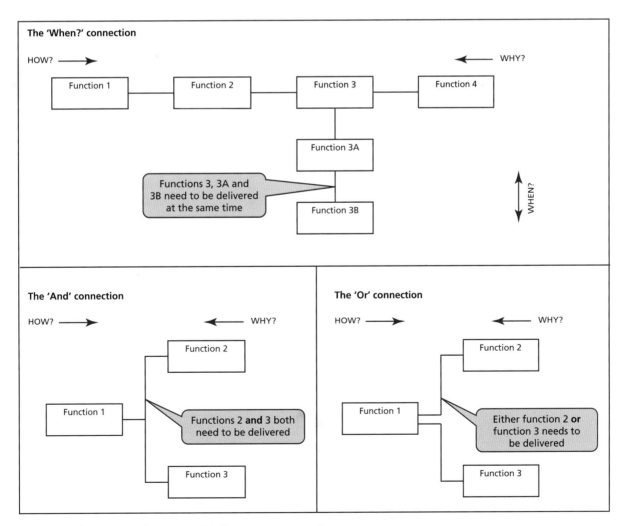

Figure 4.3 'When?', 'And' 'Or' FAST diagram connections

FAST diagrams have additional conventions, not shown in Figure 4.2:

- If two or more functions must be delivered simultaneously, a 'When?' connection will be inserted.
- If two or more lower-order functions must be satisfied for a higher-order function to be achieved, an 'and' connection will be used.
- In some cases, there is more than one way to achieve a higher-order function, in which case the 'or' connection will apply.

These connections are shown in Figure 4.3. Because a customer FAST diagram indicates a customer's expectations, the 'or' connection is not usually relevant in MoV.

Example

A contract with a government ministry involved the delivery and maintenance of multiple projects throughout the UK.

An integrated value management process was developed in collaboration with the ministry's estates department, commencing with a workshop to identify the statement of requirements for each project. A series of value management workshops then followed to explore options and select the best-value solution as the basis of the project brief and then to optimize the design to ensure that the project designed represented value for money.

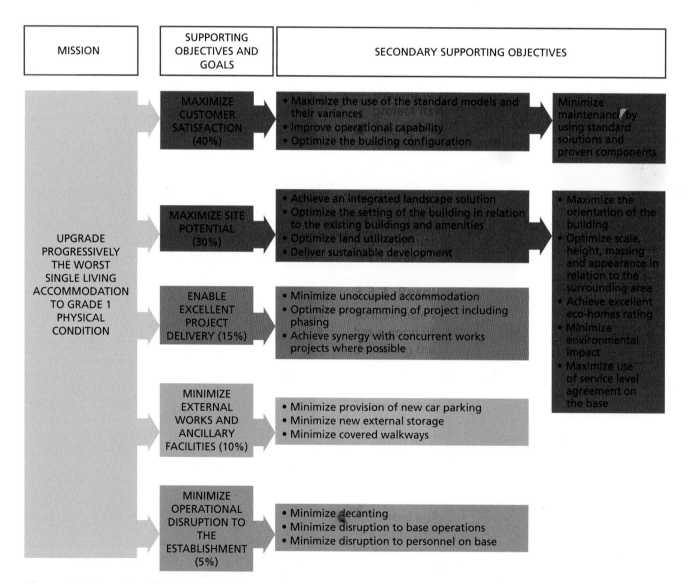

Figure 4.4 Function diagram for a government ministry contract (see example in text)

The process enabled year-on-year cost savings in addition to improvements in project delivery times and the quality of the finished buildings. The integrated value management process also reduced the amount of design iteration leading to greatly improved productivity during the design stage.

A summary of the function diagram developed for this programme is illustrated in Figure 4.4.

4.1.2 Value trees and useful derivatives

A value tree is a diagram that shows the relationship between, and the hierarchy of, value drivers. Arranging value drivers into a value tree greatly assists project team members in gaining a common understanding of the project imperatives.

Figure 4.5 illustrates a simplified value tree for a new hospital. Value drivers are normally expressed with an active verb, a qualifying adjective and a measurable noun. The project objectives should be expressed in SMART terms, that is to say: Specific,

Measurable, Achievable, Realistic and Timebound. The value tree provides a simple but precise method of conveying the function that needs to be fulfilled and also the level of quality that is required.

4.1.2.1 Value profiling

Once a value tree has been developed, it is possible to prioritize the relative importance of the primary value drivers to the client body and end users. The resulting diagram is called a value profile. This provides a powerful tool for making decisions and selecting options based on value. Because many of the judgements in prioritizing the value drivers may be subjective (albeit balanced by involvement of all key stakeholders) it is good practice to apply sensitivity analysis[6] to the finished model.

The value profile may be used to quantify value and provides a means of analysing current performance against desired performance, thus focusing attention on where effort needs to be applied to improve value.

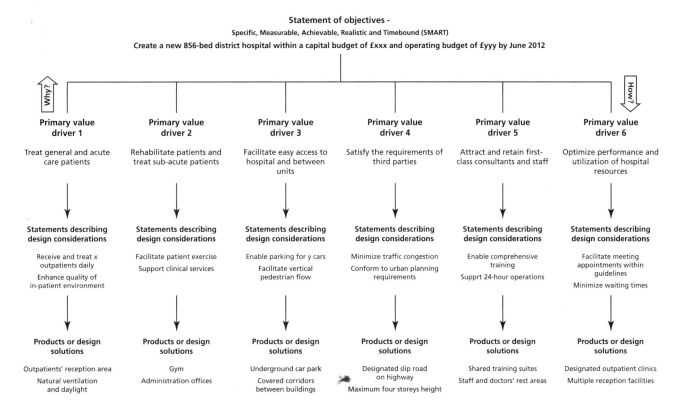

Figure 4.5 Value tree for a new hospital (simplified)

6   Sensitivity analysis involves testing the robustness of the model by varying the inputs (to reflect the risks that the assessments may not be accurate) and observing whether such variations make a significant difference to the outputs.

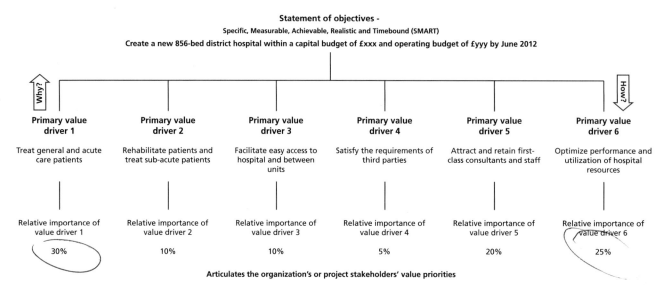

Figure 4.6   Value profile (for the same hospital as Figure 4.5)

This exercise can be conducted at any level from portfolio to project. Chapter 7 describes how establishing an organization's value profile informs the development of its MoV policy and implementation plans. An example of a project-level value profile is given in Figure 4.6.

The assessment of value priorities should be done by the programme owners or project sponsors and end users since it contributes to their organization's strategy. It should not be done by third parties such as their advisers.

Clearly, the assessment of some of the figures in a value profile can be subjective. Whilst the methods described elsewhere for achieving consensus on such figures will remove some of the subjectivity, results should always be tested for sensitivity to establish confidence in the figures.

For example:

- What is the confidence in the assessment of relative importance?
- Has the impact of potential changes in programme or project requirements been taken into account?
- What is the potential impact of foreseeable external change events?

In addition, those assessing the figures should take account of the risks that may be associated with the delivery of each value driver.

Principal uses for the value profile

- For the organization, at strategic or portfolio level, articulating the organization's value priorities
- For a programme, providing the means of achieving consistency across the contributing projects
- For a project, articulating project objectives and the key project requirements in plain language
- Maximizing value consistent with an organization's value priorities
- Making decisions based on maximizing value
- Redistributing resources to where they add the greatest value
- Trading off use of resources in one area with another to maximize value.

4.1.2.2   Simple multi-attribute rating technique

This technique uses similar logic to the value profile. It is a method of distilling meaningful measures of value by use of a 'simple, multi-attribute rating technique' or SMART (not to be confused with the identical acronym in the previous section for describing project objectives!). It combines traditional value engineering with soft-systems thinking. It is used both at the concept stage and, once the concept has been developed, later in the project lifecycle, to simplify the value tree such that value drivers are limited to those that can be measured. In the latter case, for example, it is a given that a building must conform to safety standards and so all value drivers relating to safety will be removed, as these will have to be present in all the options. Further references on SMART are given in Appendix B.

4.1.2.3 Value index

The value index provides a measure of how well an option, project or product satisfies an individual value driver or the aggregate of all value drivers. It represents a measure of customer satisfaction. Once the value profile has been formed, the team needs to agree an appropriate metric for each value driver. For some, such as 'enhance productivity', this is simple because they can be related to a tangible measure such as income. For others, such as 'satisfy community expectations', a less tangible measure such as the result of a survey may be necessary. For each metric the team needs to agree a range, from 'unacceptable' (if performance is below this level, improvements must be made or the project will fail) to 'delight' (if performance is at this level, it will satisfy the most optimistic expectations). This range, from 1 (unacceptable) to 10 (delight), provides a relatively simple method of assessing performance.

The product of the value driver weighting and the performance rating provides a number which is known as a value score. The sum of all value scores across all value drivers is the value index.

By adopting the ranges indicated above, the value index must lie between 100 and 1,000. As a rule of thumb, a value index of 350 or less indicates poor performance, which must be improved, signalling an urgent need to carry out a formal MoV study. A value index exceeding 750 is regarded as good. Perfection at 1,000 is, unfortunately, most unlikely.

Table 4.1 illustrates the calculation of the value index for the new hospital example used earlier in this chapter.

Principal uses of the value index

- Providing a measure of how well objectives are being met, at organizational, programme or project levels and the level of effort required for a formal MoV study.
- Enabling the measurement of overall value, including monetary and non-monetary value drivers (but not showing whether the benefits represent value for money).
- Indicating the contribution of each value driver to the overall value index, thus showing where to concentrate effort to improve value.

Whilst the value index demonstrates how well a project satisfies the requirements of key stakeholders (represented by the value drivers), it

Table 4.1 Value index (for the same hospital as in Figure 4.5)

Value driver	Relative importance (weight, as %)	Metric	Performance (scale of 1 to 10)	Value score (= weight × performance)
Treat general and acute care patients	30	Capacity for treating patients successfully	8	240
Rehabilitate patients and treat sub-acute patients	10	Time to appropriate discharge	5	50
Facilitate easy access to hospital and between units	10	Time to access hospital and between units	4	40
Satisfy the requirements of third parties	5	Obtaining statutory and other consents	7	35
Attract and retain first-class consultants and staff	20	Quality of facilities	6	120
Optimize performance utilization of hospital resources	25	Management procedures, departmental adjacencies and operating costs	5	125
Value index (= sum of all value scores)				**610**

does not provide any indication of whether value for money is delivered, by either the individual value drivers or by the project as a whole.

4.1.2.4 Value metrics

When setting metrics on which to assess performance or base targets, it is preferable that they should be as objective as possible and essential that existing reporting systems are capable of producing them regularly. Metrics may be set for hard and soft attributes and for monetary or non-monetary benefits.

One person should also be tasked with monitoring all metrics reported to the organization, as proliferating measures can lead to extra work without this coordination. Best results will be produced if the relationship between value drivers, or key performance indicators, and the specified measure is made clear.

In defining metrics to use against a given value driver, there is a useful checklist of questions:

■ What measurable factors influence this outcome?

■ How do changes in achievement of the value driver affect performance measures? Can these differences be detected incrementally?

■ Are any of these changes measured by other means (e.g. via a regular report that can be used for this purpose)?

Once metrics have been defined, the following process (or a similar series of steps) is very helpful in ensuring efficient monitoring:

■ State the value driver

■ Name the metric

■ Define and describe the metric

■ Name a metric owner, responsible for ensuring this data is gathered and reported

Table 4.2 The value for money ratio (for the same hospital as in Figure 4.5)

Valuedriver	Relative importance (weight, as %)	Metric	Performance (scale of 1 to 10)	Value score	Cost of delivery (£ m)	Value for money ratio (= value score or index/cost)
Treat general and acute care patients	30	Capacity for treating patients successfully	8	240	133	1.80
Rehabilitate patients and treat sub-acute patients	10	Time to appropriate discharge	5	50	60	0.83 (lowest value for money)
Facilitate easy access to hospital and between units	10	Time to access hospital and between units	4	40	30	1.33
Satisfy the requirements of third parties	5	Obtaining statutory and other consents	7	35	20	1.75
Attract and retain first-class consultants and staff	20	Quality of facilities	6	120	24	5.00
Optimize performance utilization of hospital resources	25	Management procedures, departmental adjacencies and operating costs	5	125	13	9.62 (highest value for money)
Total				**610**	**280**	**2.18**

- Describe a method of capturing the metric information
- Identify possible sources of benchmark data (this is useful for future studies)
- Report frequency
- Decide who needs to see it.

For each project type, there should be fewer than ten value drivers, so the number of metrics should be manageable. The value metrics will form part of the lessons-learned database, if there is one, in order to develop improved feedback.

Once it has been confirmed that the metric is appropriate, it can be used to measure the same value driver in future MoV studies.

4.1.2.5 Value for money ratio

The value for money ratio[7] shows an assessment of value for money, taking into account monetary and non-monetary benefits. To calculate it, the value index should be divided by the total estimated project cost, preferably in whole-life terms, to provide a value for money ratio as shown in Table 4.2. A project with a very high value index may not give best value for money if it costs significantly more than an alternative that provides only slightly lower performance.

The value for money ratios for individual value drivers provide a means of focusing MoV effort on those value drivers that provide least value for money and enable the team to redistribute resources to where they will provide greater value.

A value for money ratio can be used in option selection. It is also helpful to monitor progress during the development of a project and should be conducted at key project milestones. There is a need to ensure consistency of cost measure (here, £ m) to result in a figure that attracts the attention of senior management.

Principal uses for the value for money ratio

- Dividing individual value scores by the total cost of delivering each value driver provides a measure of value for money.

- Providing a value for money ratio for each value driver and the project as a whole helps to focus value-improving effort on those parts which are delivering lowest value for money.
- Selecting options.

> **Example**
>
> The Californian transport authority, Caltrans, regularly uses the above methods to maximize value on its infrastructure projects. In one such example, a value engineering study on the Antlers Bridge replacement project resulted in a 10% reduction in capital costs **and** a 35% increase in value, taking all factors (including operational, construction, environmental and performance) into consideration.
>
> This case study is reproduced in full in the OGC document *Value Management in Construction Case Studies*, available on the OGC website:
>
> www.ogc.gov.uk/case_studies_all_construction_case_studies

4.2 FUNCTION COST ANALYSIS

The ability to estimate the costs of value drivers (or functions), in conjunction with the relative importance of the value drivers, enables the MoV team to assess whether a particular value driver represents good value for money. Whilst fulfilling a value driver is essential to achieving the project objectives, this should not be done at any cost.

Some methods of estimating project costs are based on elemental or product costs. In such cases, one method of estimating function costs is to draw up a matrix of elemental costs on one axis and functions on the other. The total cost of each component is then distributed across the functions to which they contribute. In manufacturing and construction, the information to do this is reasonably accessible. In other situations, for example service delivery, activity-based costing[8] is needed to avoid excessive subjectivity.

E.g. Budget Airlines & Hotels.

---

7 Optimization of value for money ratio fulfils the requirement of UK's HM Treasury *Green Book* when affordability is an issue [ref clause 6.4]. If money is unlimited [ref clause 6.3] the relevant MoV measure is the value index.

8 Activity-based costing measures the cost and performance of activities, resources and the objects which that consume them in order to generate more accurate and meaningful information for decision-making. It tends to be driven by timesheets to gain a picture of activities, the time to undertake them and any other costs associated with their achievement.

Effectively, when applying costs to a function model, one is converting component cost drivers (generally arising from the use of the resources consumed in delivering them) into activity-based costs, if this is not already their format.

4.2.1 Cost/worth

Sometimes known as 'cost to function', cost/worth is a method of function analysis which examines the cost of performing each function shown in a FAST diagram. The team then decides the lowest cost at which each of the necessary functions could be performed, which is then taken as the function's worth. Comparing the current cost to the assigned worth reveals subjects for further discussion. The cost of performing each function is estimated from the cost of the elements or products that are necessary to deliver the function. There is a risk that if a function is taken in isolation, it may lead to unacceptable cost-cutting. This is because some of the supporting functions must also be delivered to meet customers' needs.

The most effective way to avoid the risk of inappropriate cost-cutting leading to value reduction is to apply costs to a full function diagram, where all relationships will be more apparent.

4.3 VALUE ENGINEERING/ANALYSIS

This is a defined application of recognized techniques for generating alternative actions to improve value through balancing function and cost without detriment to quality. It is sometimes also called value analysis.[9]

Value engineering (VE) is a method that brings many of the above processes together into one coordinated study. It is the original process introduced in the USA shortly after the Second World War and, whilst it too has evolved in sophistication, it remains the most commonly used method within the MoV family.

Its primary purpose is to improve value in an existing design or set of circumstances by studying in detail two fundamental questions:

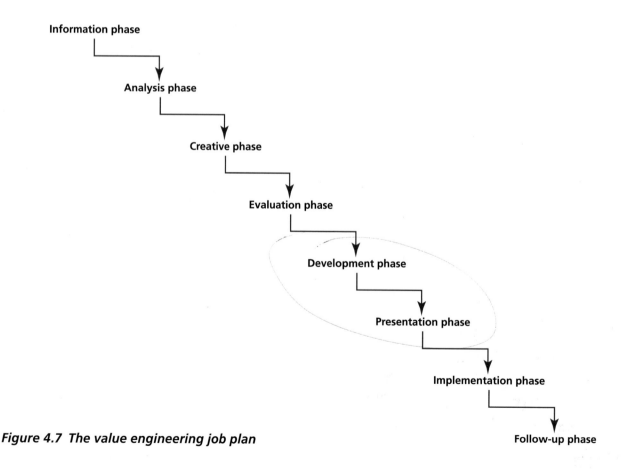

Figure 4.7 The value engineering job plan

---

9   Some literature draws a distinction between value engineering and value analysis, the former being applied to improve evolving designs and the latter being applied to improve existing products. The process for each is the same.

- What functions must be delivered?
- How else can they be performed?

VE comprises eight steps, usually referred to as phases. Together they form the VE job plan illustrated in Figure 4.7.

The VE study will be arranged and facilitated by a skilled study leader and normally comprises a period of gathering and analysing information before convening a workshop at which all key project stakeholders will be present. At the end of the workshop or shortly thereafter, the team will present their findings and recommendations to a decision-making panel and agree an implementation plan. Value-improving proposals will then be implemented by the project team.

4.3.1 Information phase

This initial phase contains all of the processes discussed in section 3.2. It is initiated by a meeting with a few key stakeholders to gain an understanding of the project in question, the challenges faced, the purpose of the study, those who should be present, and other logistical details. This meeting may be run in workshop format and is often named the 'pre-event'. If the information needed is not available at this initial meeting, the study leader will gather it over the next few days, whilst also arranging the venue and inviting participants to the workshop.

4.3.2 Analysis phase

This phase is started before the workshop and completed during it. It contains many of the processes given under section 3.3. Before the workshop, the study leader will review the information and ensure that it is consistent and up to date. This may involve reconciling differences between, for example, drawings and cost estimates. Items that will aid the workshop team's understanding of the issues involved, such as cost models, are prepared. It is also possible to prepare a draft function analysis in advance of the workshop, although this is ideally done with the team. The latter approach, although it extends the workshop duration, ensures that all workshop team members have the opportunity to contribute fully to its creation, thus increasing their buy-in and understanding of the functions that drive the project. The study leader will, with assistance from the project cost analysts, allocate costs to the function model if appropriate or practical.

Function analysis identifies four classes of potential value mismatches:

- Those functions which add cost but do not add to stakeholder benefits – delete if possible or minimize
- Those functions that add appropriate stakeholder benefits but at an excessive cost – reduce cost
- Those functions that do not perform adequately to meet stakeholder benefits – improve
- Required stakeholder benefits that are not being met – create functions to fill the shortcomings.

A workshop handbook is prepared by the study leader to guide all workshop team members through the workshop processes. At the beginning of the workshop the study leader will brief the team as to what to expect during the workshop and the roles they need to play, if this has not already been done in the information phase. Key project team members brief the team on any new information and the issues to be addressed.

4.3.3 Creative (or speculation) phase

Using the function (cost) analysis as a framework, the study leader will first invite the workshop team to highlight any areas of the project that hold particular potential for value improvement. The study leader then conducts a creative session with the team, usually through brainstorming, to capture as many ideas as possible for improving value.

4.3.4 Evaluation phase

The workshop team will then use the methods described later in this chapter to evaluate the ideas and select those that warrant further effort to develop into value-improving proposals.

4.3.5 Development phase

Either during the workshop or immediately after it, the workshop team will take the selected ideas and develop them into full value-improving proposals.

4.3.6 Presentation phase

The team will present their recommendations to a decision-making panel to agree which should be included in the project and agree an implementation plan. This session is chaired by the

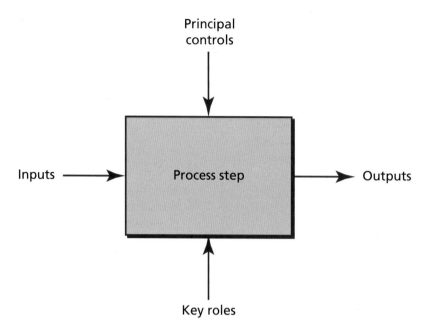

Figure 4.8 Typical process step

study leader and attended by the workshop team who developed the proposals. These processes are described in section 3.7 of this guide.

4.3.7 Implementation phase

After the agreement of the implementation plan, the study leader will compile a report on the VE study as a record of the event and a guide for the project team who will implement the value-improving proposals.

4.3.8 Follow-up phase

The full benefits arising from the VE study will only be realized if the implementation plan is rigorously followed through, progress monitored and appropriate remedial action taken if expectations are not being realized.

4.4 TECHNIQUES COMMONLY USED IN MoV *(Not exhaustive)*

4.4.1 Information analysis

4.4.1.1 Benchmarking

This is defined as comparing performance or cost of an attribute of a project (or process) with other examples with similar characteristics. It is very useful to focus on anomalies identified by this process to define whether good value is being delivered or not.

There are many sources of information on techniques in this field. It is worth noting that, whilst any external comparison will be very informative, benchmarking exclusively with same-type organizations can mask opportunities for innovation. Benchmarking against a wider pool of other industries whose only common feature lies in the type of process being compared can yield some startling results.

4.4.1.2 Process mapping

Process mapping provides a method for understanding what is 'business as usual' and then illustrating potential future alternatives. It is particularly useful for representing processes diagrammatically to aid understanding in MoV studies aimed at improving operational efficiency. Different methods tend to emphasize different aspects of a process – for example responsibilities, information flows and product stages.

For each step in the process the analyst needs to understand information flows, roles, responsibilities and controls, an approximation of the resources it uses and the outputs that indicate the purposes which the process step serves (see Figure 4.8). Each process step may then be linked in a logical manner to provide a map of the whole process. Some processes may stretch beyond the organization and external parties will have to be involved in the mapping activity.

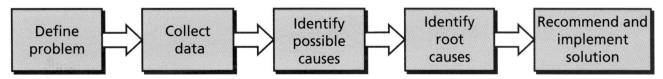

Figure 4.9 Root cause analysis

4.4.1.3 Root cause analysis

Root cause analysis is a combination of several techniques aimed at drilling down to the root of a problem in order to develop an appropriate solution. It involves five steps (see Figure 4.9). Repeated use of the question 'Why?' provides a rapid way to establish the root cause of a problem.

Root cause analysis focuses on underlying issues, rather than solving specific problems. It can be applied to a number of situations: for example, in improving processes, it will find unnecessary constraints and inadequate controls; in risk management, it can find unrecognized hazards. The technique can provide vital information on what needs changing and how to change it. It is helpful to quantify the impact of the problem. This provides a measure of the realizable benefit if the problem is resolved and assists in prioritizing where the effort should be applied.

The steps shown in Figure 4.9 can be undertaken in a number of ways, including use of 'five whys' (repeated use of the question 'Why' provides a rapid way to establish the root cause of a problem) and 'fishbone analysis' (which analyses a given problem under the headings of all factors affecting it). In both cases, a hierarchy of causes and effects can be established as a focus for developing improvements.

4.4.1.4 Discounted cash flow analysis

Discounted cash flow (DCF) analysis is a method of expressing future cash flows at current equivalent values. These flows can be sales, interest or dividends. The basic calculation is made by reference to the following formula:

$$\text{Net present value} = \frac{\text{cash flow}}{(1+r)^n}$$

where r is the discount rate and n the number of years.

This is normally the rate of inflation, but sometimes is a hurdle rate used within an organization.

There are many methods, but all do the same thing, which is to estimate the return on investment adjusted for the effect of time.

In any project there are three types of cost to be considered:

- Capital or one-off costs required to purchase the resources used to deliver the project.
- Periodic costs incurred in maintaining or replacing things once the project is complete and in use.
- Regular costs such as staff or consumables for operations.

When calculating the total cost of a project, these cannot be simply added together. DCF provides a method of calculating the total costs of a capital investment as it takes account of present and future cash flows. DCF may be used for estimating the net present value (NPV) of future cash flows. The present value (PV) of future cash flows will be heavily influenced by the discount rate applied, as the higher the rate the lower the value of future cash flows. The appropriate discount rate must be agreed with the project executive or manager. The PV for each cash flow may then be added to capital costs to arrive at the total net present value.

Care must be taken when estimating future cash flows since these are notoriously unreliable. (Who can forecast the cost of staff employment in ten years' time with any accuracy?) Small changes in cash flow and the discount rate used can result in large differences in the final NPV. For this reason, DCF is usually used for a relatively short finite period, rather than just continuing to zero.

This method should be used when evaluating all value-improving proposals where the benefits are monetary, for example:

- The proposal may result in positive or negative future cash flows
- Comparison between alternative investments or projects is needed
- Comparison is made between alternative investments or projects which have differing cash flow timing.

The technique may be used in conjunction with the value index to take account of non-monetary benefits as well as monetary benefits. Ideally the costs used in calculating the value for money ratio should be expressed in NPV terms, but this is not always practical.

4.4.2 Idea generation

4.4.2.1 Brainstorming

Also known as braindumping, boardstorming, mind showering – this involves encouraging people to think up an idea and share it without prejudice. The method is capable of generating a large number of ways to improve value, varying in merit.

The study leader simply invites team members to come up with solutions and records these ideas in the originator's own words in a way visible to all team members. By keeping ideas visible, other possibilities may be sparked off in people's minds. This visibility of output helps generate further ideas, sometimes later in the session. Additional solutions can also be added outside the workshop and still be included in the total for the study. Brainstorming can generate a large volume of ideas in a short period of time and will generally ensure that all parties are involved.

The function analysis model selected by the project should be used as a guide to ensure that all eligible areas for improvement are brainstormed. Focusing on other ways to perform functions also leads to more innovation than focusing on products. Sometimes it can help to give some guidelines for this – e.g. how can we satisfy two functions in one process?

Care must be taken not to discount any idea, no matter how foolish it appears at first. A unique identifier must be given to each proposal: this is essential to permit the tracking of suggestions from inception to implementation and also for use by future workshops. Although an idea may not be practicable at the time, if the situation changes in the future it could be developed into a very effective solution.

References to other creative techniques are provided in Appendix B.

4.4.3 Evaluation and option selection

The following techniques provide ways to select the most advantageous ideas from a number that may have been generated during the idea generation stages of an MoV study.

4.4.3.1 Option evaluation matrix

The value profile provides an excellent way to assess the merits of different options using an option evaluation matrix (see Table 4.3). This method is appropriate where there are a small number of options from which to choose.

The relative performance of each option against the weighted primary value drivers is assessed by the MoV team. This enables calculation of a value score for each option, the highest score indicating the option that best satisfies the project objectives (represented by the weighted value drivers). Division of the value score by the cost of delivering the option provides a measure of value for money known as the value index. The option resulting in the highest value index is likely to provide the best value for money.

The above analysis needs to be reviewed carefully and tested for sensitivity in assessing the performance of each option against the value drivers, since this may be subjective. The results of this method should be regarded as a guide to selection and further validated by other methods.

A form for an option evaluation matrix is given in Appendix A. A simplified example of the use of this form is given in Table 4.3.

The following six actions should be considered before reaching the option selection stage of a given study:

- Select criteria (usually the primary value drivers)
- Define scale of improvement required and sensitivity ranges
- Establish weights for relative importance
- Rank the benefit of each option against the criteria
- Calculate benefit ranking × weight
- Apply sensitivity analysis to confirm robustness of value index.

The most feasible options in terms of costs, benefits and risks are presented for decision during the decision-building meeting. In this meeting, the owner of each idea or scenario presents their proposal to those with decision-making power. This ensures ownership of the idea and its implementation, if agreed. The recommendation will include a detailed description of both the existing situation and the solution, together with advantages and drawbacks of all the alternatives considered. Each of these will show assessed impacts

Table 4.3 An example of an option evaluation matrix

No.	Option (and cost)	Criterion weight	Criterion 1	Criterion 2	Criterion 3	Criterion 4	Criterion 5	Criterion 6	Criterion 7	Criterion 8	Total	Measure of value for money
			Evaluation criteria (i.e. value drivers)									
			25%	10%	10%	5%	20%	20%	5%	5%		
1	Option A (cost = 100)	Benefit ranking	2	3	4	2	3	4	2	2		
		Benefit ranking × criterion weight	50	30	40	10	60	80	10	10	290	2.90
2	Option B (cost = 125)	Benefit Ranking	3	2	4	1	2	3	3	2		
		Benefit ranking × criterion weight	75	20	40	5	40	60	15	10	265	2.12
3	Option C (cost = 150)	Benefit ranking	4	2	3	3	3	4	2	3		
		Benefit ranking × criterion weight	100	20	30	15	60	80	10	15	330	2.20
		Benefit ranking: 1= poor; 2= Fair; 3= Good; 4= Excellent										

in terms of cost, time and quality: there is a checklist in Appendix A for a value-improving proposal development form to ensure completeness. The owner will describe the implementation plan.

4.4.3.2 Allocation to categories

Where there are a large number of ideas from which to select, an effective technique is to identify a number of criteria against which each idea is assessed. In the resulting discussion, the study leader will broker a consensus with the MoV team to categorize each idea. Typical categories might be:

- Unanimous agreement that the idea warrants further development starting now.
- The idea has potential but there is insufficient information to develop it now. It requires further research or testing.
- The idea has potential but cannot, for reasons which should be recorded, be developed in this project. Record the idea for possible use in other similar projects.
- The idea is not appropriate and should be discarded.

This technique is quick and allows plenty of discussion around the merits and demerits of the idea, which promotes sound selection.

If it is so easy why have we not done it?

Why is it novel – what do we need to do?

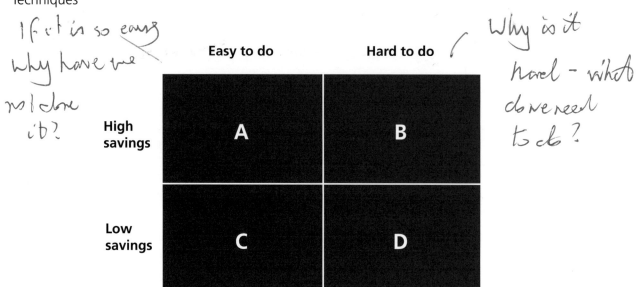

Easy to do   Hard to do

High savings   A   B

Low savings   C   D

Figure 4.10 Idea selection matrix

4.4.3.3 Idea selection matrix

An even quicker way to select the most promising ideas from a large number of suggestions is to use a selection matrix (see Figure 4.10).

The axes of the matrix reflect the grounds on which decisions will be based, for example easy or hard to implement with high or low cost savings.

Ideas are placed in one of the four quadrants of the matrix.

Clearly, ideas that are easy to implement and result in high cost savings will normally warrant development. Those that are easy to develop and result in low cost savings may be worth the effort to develop. Likewise those that are hard to implement but could result in high savings may also warrant development. Those that are hard to implement and would result in low savings are unlikely to be worth developing.

4.4.4 Weighting techniques

In order to prioritize value drivers, it is necessary to have an objective method of weighting them. It is important to choose a method that minimizes the contributors' ability to bias the results.

All weighting methods involve a measure of subjectivity and should therefore be used as a guide to decision-making rather than be interpreted as fact.

4.4.4.1 Paired comparisons

This method ranks items by comparing all possible pairs in a given list of attributes and selecting one from each pair at each comparison. It enables option selection and alternatives to be reviewed in order to support decision-making. This technique requires that team members compare the relative performance of two items at a time, creating a chart of all responses and totalling the results (see Figure 4.11). These results are then translated into percentages. This method provides a robust and reasonably objective means of assessing the relative weighting of attributes. Whilst it can be quite time-consuming to implement, it is highly effective in achieving consensus.

4.4.4.2 Points distribution

The team is given 100 points to allocate between ideas. The total points allocated are divided by the number of contributors and then converted to percentage weightings for each.

Care must be taken that the contributors are truly representative of all decision-makers. For this reason, the study leader needs to agree on a fair representation for each stakeholder before starting the comparison.

If individual weightings are very disparate, the average cannot be taken as representative and a convergence tool, such as Delphi,[10] should then be used.

---

10 Delphi is a technique in which if there is significant disparity between contributors' assessments of certain variables, they will discuss the reasons for their individual assessments. Having heard the arguments put forward by others they will reassess the variables. This usually leads to consensus after a few iterations. Further references to the Delphi technique are signposted in Appendix B.

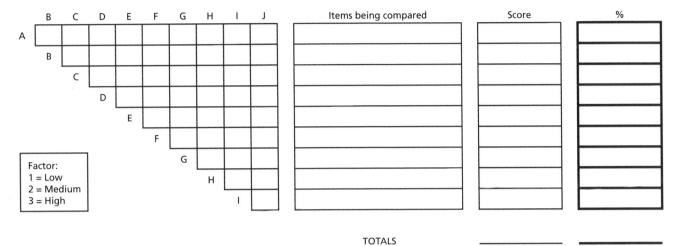

Figure 4.11 Paired comparison matrix

4.4.5 Developing value-improving proposals

The outputs from the selection techniques above will be a list of ideas or options that warrant development into a detailed value-improving proposal (VIP). It is the responsibility of the owner of each selected idea or option (allocated during the selection process) to develop each proposal.

These should be summarized in a standard format, such as that provided in Appendix A, which contains all the information needed for the decision makers to exercise their judgement as to whether to implement the VIP in total, partially or not at all.

4.4.5.1 Cost benefit analysis

This is a method of assessing the cost of implementing a proposal against the benefits it will deliver over the long term. Normally used in conjunction with discounted cash flow, it assists business case decisions. Often used in MoV in studies of process or procedure, it can be combined with many other tools, e.g. process mapping and option selection.

In the UK, the approach to cost benefit analysis (CBA) in central government is set out in HM Treasury's *Green Book*, which recommends that 'all new policies, programmes and projects … should be subject to comprehensive but proportionate assessment, wherever it is practicable, so as best to promote the public interest.'

4.4.5.2 Decision-building meeting

The study leader should convene and chair a decision-building meeting at which proposal owners present their suggestions to a panel of senior managers. The purpose of this meeting is to discuss the findings of each proposal and agree whether or not it should be implemented in whole or in part. Each of the value-improving proposals selected for implementation is allocated to an owner who is responsible for its implementation.

The decisions are recorded and form the basis of the proposal implementation plan. This plan provides the project managers with details of proposals, how and when they will be implemented and the expected value improvements (or benefits). This allows them to monitor and manage the implementation process (described in section 3.7).

4.4.6 Implementing VIPs and follow-up

4.4.6.1 Implementation plans

Once the value-improving proposal form has been presented and accepted for further development, a method is needed for the study team to implement its value enhancement. At this stage, there are usually some guesstimates in cost benefit values, and the practicalities of a delivery plan may not be fully considered. It may therefore be necessary to add another step to the process.

Building on the value-improving proposal form template given in Appendix A, the proposal owner will need (in liaison with the study leader as coordinator, as there will be other proposal owners) to:

■ Revisit the proposal to ensure that claimed advantages, drawbacks and cost calculations are robust

■ Develop an implementation plan, with assigned human resources

- Draw up a timetable for delivery, giving milestones as appropriate
- Agree the progress-reporting schedule.

The proposal owners are responsible for ensuring that their proposals are implemented. The project executive or manager should take overall responsibility for their implementation. Regular progress reports should be included as part of the overall project-reporting system.

4.4.6.2 Feedback

The MoV study report and regular updates feed back lessons learned (both for the MoV approach taken to a project and for the outcomes it provides). This feedback can be communicated as appropriate across the organization.

Involving people from across the organization and externally is a key strength of MoV: the best solutions to a given topic come from involving all relevant disciplines. Their positive contribution is essential and they should not merely become involved because it makes a change from normal day-to-day activities. The study leader must make it clear to the study team what they need to do, the study objectives, what may and what may not be challenged and the processes to be used. The study handbook will explain to them the resources that will be available, the timetable and the agenda for the study. If required, participants will be trained in the process, at least to awareness level, so that they can contribute fully. This applies equally to staff, consultants, suppliers and other stakeholders. The improved communication flowing from this collaborative work not only enhances the effectiveness of MoV in the study but will also have long-term benefits for the organization in building an appropriate culture.

4.4.6.3 Tracking benefits

It is worth noting that improvements arising from MoV proposals may need to be monitored for a considerable length of time, so that individual benefits can be clearly tracked, quantified and communicated to the organization. Whether this activity is managed via a benefits realization plan or simply via the regular MoV report, the method of monitoring and metric used must be sufficiently objective to stand up to independent review.

Approach to implementation

5

5 Approach to implementation

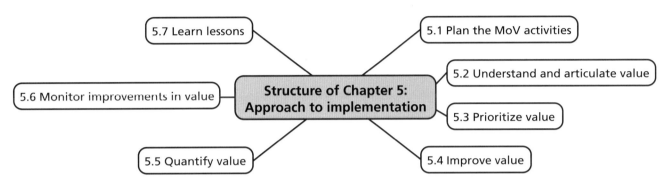

Figure 5.1 Structure of Chapter 5

The approach taken in implementing MoV for a project should be scaled to suit the size and complexity of the challenges presented.

Chapter 3 summarized the processes to be followed in MoV. This chapter explains the purpose of following the processes and sets out a generic approach around which the study leader can structure the detailed MoV programme or project strategy (see Figure 5.1). Extension across a portfolio of programmes will add value at enterprise level.

Smaller organizations, or cases where an MoV is being applied to a single project, may not require every detail set out below and should adjust their approach accordingly.

5.1 PLAN THE MoV ACTIVITIES

All programmes and projects are different and will require the development of a specific MoV programme or project plan (hereafter in this chapter called the plan). The plan should reflect the stages of the project at which MoV is applied as well as its scale and complexity (see sections 2.4 and 2.5).

5.1.1 The MoV project plan

Figure 5.2 illustrates a generic plan that is applicable at any stage in the project and is appropriate for any MoV activity.

The first step (1) is to define what it is you are seeking to do (the MoV study objectives) and then select the appropriate methods and tools to achieve the objectives.

Having identified the objectives of the MoV study (or review in the event of a study having already taken place) at this stage in the project, the next step (2) is to ascertain who is affected and who should be on the MoV team tasked with achieving the study objectives. It may be appropriate to quantify any targets that need to be achieved at this point or be left until later (see step 9).

The next step (3) is to identify the most appropriate MoV methods to apply. Having selected the appropriate methods, it may be necessary to provide awareness training (step 4) to the people who will be involved in the review so that they can contribute effectively.

Having gathered information on the project (step 5), the next step (6) is to articulate the project objectives and the value drivers (or key functions) that must be fulfilled. This process is termed 'function analysis' and several methods are offered in Chapter 4. It forms a core of any subsequent course of action aimed at improving value.

At this point the MoV study leader should work with the project sponsor and/or end users to prioritize the value drivers (step 7) and establish appropriate metrics for each to measure the project's performance against them (step 8). If targets and measures have not been set earlier, they should be set now (step 9).

Applying the methods identified in step 3 will enable the study team to arrive at recommendations for adding value (step 10). These are usually referred to as value-improving proposals. Proposals that are accepted by management will then be

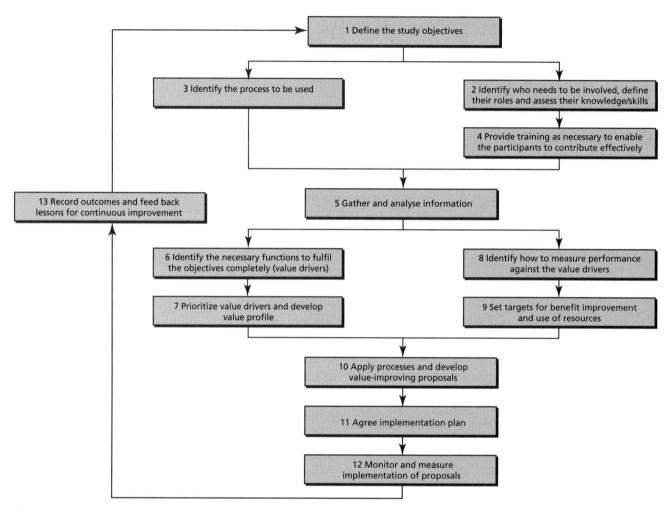

Figure 5.2 Generic MoV project plan

implemented in accordance with an implementation plan (step 11) and their progress monitored and reported (step 12).

Throughout the project and when it is completed, the MoV study leader will record the outputs from each MoV activity and provide feedback to enable continuous improvement (step 13).

Where a project forms part of a wider programme, it may be appropriate to have separate plans for each project, all of which are linked to an overall programme plan (see Figure 5.3). If MoV has been embedded within the organization undertaking the project, these plans should be consistent with the organization's overall MoV policy and MoV implementation strategy.

Example

A wind turbine manufacturer undertook an extensive MoV programme to improve its competiveness. The programme involve numerous studies, divided into six workstreams, to improve different aspects of the end-to-end activities for making the components, shipping them to site, installing and maintaining them.

The MoV study teams had never undertaken MoV studies before and came from three separate countries in Europe. In order to maximize their abilities to contribute effectively to the studies, each workstream team was given familiarization training in MoV techniques. The output of the programme was the identification of opportunities to reduce the cost per unit of electricity generated by 30%.

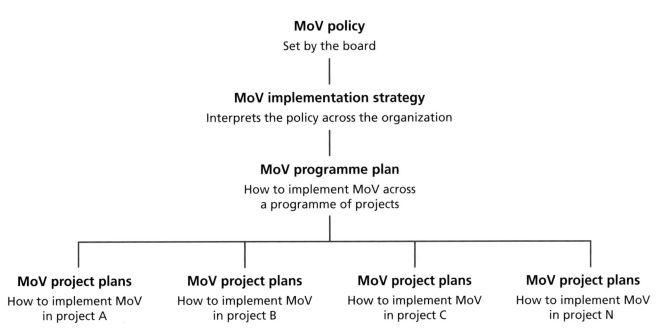

Figure 5.3 Integrated programme and project plans

Where projects do not form part of a wider programme, this integration is unnecessary. Nor will it be needed if the organization undertaking the project has not embedded MoV. Conversely, if the programme forms part of an enterprise-wide portfolio, the model in Figure 5.3 should be extended to show the programmes included within the portfolio.

5.1.2 Programme or project organization

To manage the MoV activities it will be necessary to have some form of organization in place. The extent of this organization will be dependent upon the following variables:

- The scale and complexity of the programme or project
- The size of the organization undertaking the project
- Whether MoV is being applied to a project in isolation or as part of a wider programme.

The organization that has embedded MoV in its processes can draw its MoV study leader from within the organization. Smaller organizations, or projects where MoV is being applied on a one-off basis, may choose to acquire MoV expertise from third parties.

In either case the MoV study leaders should be independent of the project teams to ensure full examination of all relevant issues and lack of personal bias. The relationship between the MoV practitioners and the project teams is illustrated in Figure 5.4.

Figure 5.4 shows the organization for the full embedding of MoV in a large organization. For the smaller organization, or if MoV is being applied on a project-by-project basis using external resource, the roles may be undertaken by existing management and staff as part of their day-to-day duties.

5.1.3 Integrated MoV study team

An MoV study team will typically comprise an MoV study leader (often assisted by a recorder or scribe to gather and maintain accurate records of proceedings) together with a representative selection of members of the project team and relevant stakeholders.

One of MoV's strengths is its ability to harness people's strengths and talents to create solutions that none would have reached individually. It therefore has great motivational power to encourage team members to raise their game to improve performance. MoV does this by ensuring that teams are a carefully selected diverse mix of all those who will have a stake in the outcome of the MoV activities, allowing them to reach an understanding of each other's issues and to value their knowledge and experience in reaching study objectives. It also ensures that they understand clearly how the study objectives link to those of the organization, helping them to step outside their comfort zones.

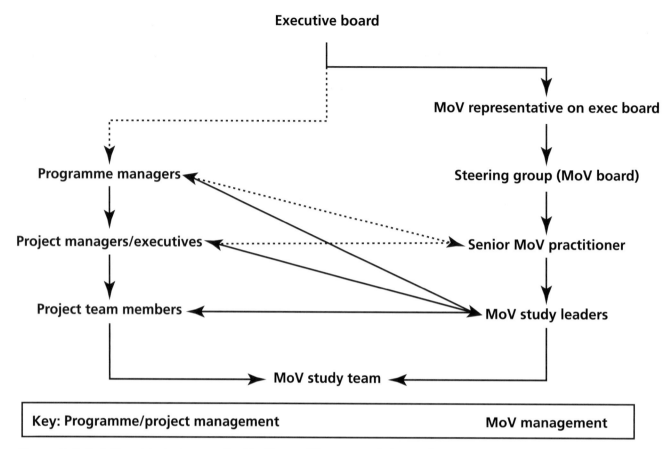

Figure 5.4 Relationship between the MoV practitioners and the project team

Care is needed to ensure the study team is able to break into small groups to permit close relationships to be formed, whilst still maintaining the completeness of perspective that permits valuable creative synergy. As familiarity with the MoV study process and other team members increases, so collaboration and effectiveness will improve.

5.1.4 Planning for use throughout the project

MoV activities should be planned from project start up to take place throughout the life of the project. Formal studies should be planned to inform key decision points.

Table 5.1 indicates the stages at which a formal MoV study is recommended, the focus of the study and the nature of the outputs from it. The project stages indicated are intended to be generic rather than related to any particular sector.

Whilst the table implies a series of discrete events, it is intended to indicate the key stages at which a formal MoV study may be considered, not all of which will be relevant for every project. MoV works best when it runs continuously throughout a project, so that realization of added value is monitored and there is a constant review to check that proposals are aligned with value delivery. While MoV can pick up on the focus areas as shown, the value drivers and value tree (see below) should be carried forward and developed further at each stage so that future decisions are taken with an understanding of past decisions. This will alert the team to any changes in the project that may have evolved. At the end of the project, the team should review the effectiveness of the MoV process and feed lessons learned back to the senior MoV practitioner and, if appropriate, MoV steering group or board.

Although described above as a continuous progression, frequently it will be necessary to revisit an earlier stage because conditions have changed, or because a proposed course of action proves impractical.

MoV is particularly important at project start up, at stage boundaries and to inform other key decision points.

Table 5.1 MoV at key project stages

PRINCE2 stages	Gateways	Traditional project stages	Focus of MoV study	Main study output
Start up	Gateway 0: strategic assessment	Inception	Validate need for project	Information to improve the business case
Authority to initiate	Gateway 1: business justification			
Initiate project	Gateway 2: delivery strategy	Concept	Project definition	Functional definition of project
Authority to deliver	Gateway 3: investment decision	Feasibility (note: PRINCE2 can treat this as a separate project)	Assess options	Information to clarify a viable brief
Delivery stages	Gateway 5: operational reviews and benefits realization	Design Implementation Completion	Balance benefits and resources Delivery processes Review outcomes	Maximized value Optimized delivery Lessons learned for continuous improvement
Authority to close	Gateway readiness for service			
Post-project review	Gateway 5: operational reviews and benefits realization	Use	Review outcomes Improve operations	Improved operational efficiency

In a programme of projects, lessons learned from one project should be communicated to the other projects within the programme, which may be at different stages of development. These lessons should also be communicated to the operational teams during business as usual so that they can maintain the value added. MoV between each project will be coordinated by applying the overall programme value drivers to each project, providing the means to assess the value added by each project to the programme, as well as harmonizing the approach taken by each project (see example in section 2.1).

Example

A defence programme comprised more than 70 separate, but similar, phased projects throughout the UK. Lessons learned from MoV on the first few projects to be implemented allowed subsequent projects to be delivered more quickly, with fewer problems and at reduced cost.

As indicated earlier, MoV may be introduced either from the top down or the bottom up. For example, it may be desirable to apply MoV to a project independently, whether it is part of a wider programme or not. This might be the case for a single project within a smaller organization or it might be part of a trial to convince senior management to implement MoV across a wider programme.

The diagram in Figure 5.5 illustrates how MoV may be applied at portfolio level to include several programmes if these form part of an enterprise-wide portfolio.

There is often an opportunity to improve the efficiency, economy and effectiveness of operations, generally in the following circumstances:

■ When there is a change in customer profile (or other external factor) requiring reassessment of the service provided.

■ On completion of a project, whether IT or infrastructure, to harness full advantage from investment. Once a project is completed, it passes to the operational or 'business as usual' phase. MoV has a role to play in ensuring that the transition from project to operational phase is conducted as smoothly and effectively as possible, thus avoiding disruption (which destroys value). Once normal operations are

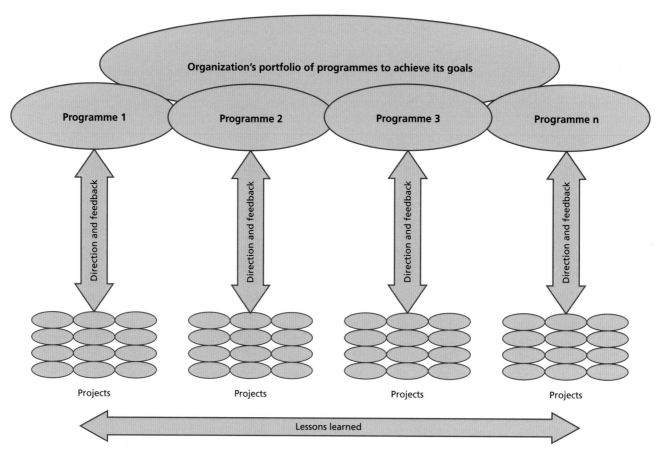

Figure 5.5 MoV applied at portfolio level

established, all MoV projects should have a 'business as usual' appraisal, or post-project review, to establish whether expected benefits have materialized and to explore opportunities to improve operational efficiency.

■ As part of a continuous improvement programme.

■ When there is a requirement to deliver more for less because of budget constraints.

MoV can be applied very effectively to bring about significant improvements in any of these.

Example

A London borough undertook a review of its maintenance services division to improve productivity using the MoV approach. Staff, shop floor workers, supervisors and managers all worked collaboratively to bring about a 15% improvement in productivity through smarter ways of working, with no loss of staff.

5.2 UNDERSTAND AND ARTICULATE VALUE

5.2.1 Align with organizational objectives

An underlying principle of MoV is that all activities must be aligned with the objectives of the organization. This is illustrated by the value cascade shown in Figure 5.6, on which are superimposed the concepts of PRINCE2 and MSP.

This diagram shows that every component or product which forms part of a project must be there for a reason that ultimately contributes to the overall organizational objectives, which are themselves reflective of the organization's aspirations and values.

Where projects are part of a programme, these are put together in order to fulfil an organizational objective, or portfolio vision and blueprint. Each project within the programme is designed to contribute directly or indirectly to achieving the programme outcomes. Each project should also be complementary to the other projects within the programme, ideally without overlapping objectives.

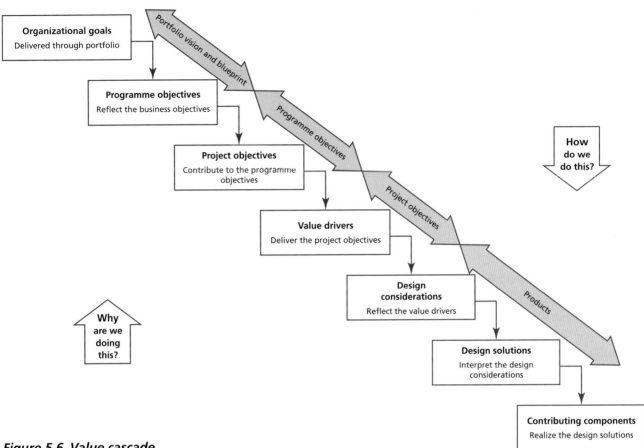

Figure 5.6 Value cascade

Example

MoV was a key enabler in delivering timely progress and value for money for a £5 billion investment in housing services over seven years. National legislation introduced a new duty on local government to develop housing policy and local housing strategy to implement that policy. MoV principles, processes, techniques and approach to implementation were applied to deliver policy option appraisals, stimulate public engagement and debate, and develop local housing strategies for every local authority in the country. Specific local programmes and projects were then delivered using MoV to improve social housing services and the standard of public and private housing stock through staff development, organizational change, and contract procurement.

In order that each project delivers its outputs in full, the project team must deliver a number of primary functions, the sum of which will be necessary and sufficient to deliver these outputs. In MoV, these primary functions may be called 'value drivers', as explained in Chapter 2.

In turn, these inform what the designers need to take into consideration when developing their proposals for implementing the project. Their knowledge of the situation and the skills they bring to it allow them to contribute to the development of the design brief. MoV ensures that the designers are working to the same priorities to arrive at solutions which, together, will fulfil the requirements of the completed project. Each of the design solutions will be built up from a number of parts, or products, selected in accordance with the requirements of the design brief.

Under MoV, if a part or element is not contributing effectively to the design solution, an alternative will be sought that fulfils its function more effectively. If its function is unnecessary, it may be eliminated.

The broader the focus of objectives, the greater the opportunity there is to enhance value. For example, at programme level, the focus of MoV activity will be to explore alternative projects to fulfil the programme outcome. In this way, MoV can be seen to support management in making better decisions.

Example

In a classic 'make or buy' situation, a chemical manufacturer was seeking to double production of a product. The proposed solution was to expand its existing manufacturing facilities. An exploration of the possible alternatives, using MoV, demonstrated that a better solution was to outsource additional manufacture in conjunction with risk analysis. This provided far greater value enhancement than if the company had focused its efforts on improving its existing facilities or had streamlined the design of the proposed new facilities.

5.2.2 Articulate value

MoV uses the concept of function analysis to articulate value. The techniques of function analysis are explained in Chapter 4. The use of value trees is particularly recommended as it provides a simple method of articulating value in plain language that all can understand.

To recap, a value tree arranges value drivers in a diagram that illustrates their relationship to the required project objectives. The relationship between value drivers is ascertained by asking the questions 'How?' and 'Why?' If all value drivers are delivered in full, all the project objectives will be met. If any fall short, they won't.

Most sectors and disciplines have developed their own technical language and culture, often referred to as jargon. For MoV to be effective, it is vital that study leaders understand the business in which they are operating as well as the technical language. The following guidelines may be useful to gain a better understanding of an organization's business:

- Terminology – understand the organization's jargon
- Culture – understand the organization's value profile
- Technical expertise – understand what the organization does
- Business drivers – understand the organization's priorities, e.g. their market proposition. This may also be reflected in the value profile.

5.3 PRIORITIZE VALUE

All value drivers are important and must be delivered in full for a successful outcome. However, in most cases, some are more important than others. Adding a measure of the relative importance of each value driver, usually in percentage terms, produces a value profile. Methods of assessing the relative importance of various attributes are given in Chapter 4 and Appendix B. This exercise should be conducted with the owners of the project and its end users, rather than the project delivery team, since it is the owners and end users who will use the completed project in the long term.

As the relative importance of value drivers will vary on different projects, distinctions can more easily be made where the projects are apparently similar. For example, if the required output of a project is to establish a retail operation, speed of delivery may be the most important value driver. If the output of the project is to safeguard health, compliance with health and safety requirements may be more important than speed of delivery.

A clear statement of the relative importance of individual value drivers makes it possible to maximize value in a way that is consistent with the organization's or the project's overall objectives. The value profile also provides the basis for making decisions based upon value and of quantifying the value added to or expected from a project, however this is judged. It may be used to assess value in a way that takes into account both monetary and non-monetary value drivers, thus providing a means of measuring performance against each.

5.4 IMPROVE VALUE

The development of function models such as those illustrated in the above sections provides the key to making improvements in value in an innovative manner. Instead of focusing on products and asking the question 'What other product would be acceptable?' the MoV study team can ask 'How else can we perform the required function?' This change of emphasis opens the way to all manner of alternatives which might bear no relation to the product initially envisaged. Asking this question in relation to the higher-order value drivers (or functions) can significantly alter the nature of the solutions whilst still delivering the required functionality. This can lead to step changes in value improvement.

5.4.1 Redistributing resources to maximize value

The value profile can be used to redistribute resources in a project to where they create the greatest value. The cost of delivering each value driver may be estimated using function cost analysis (described in Chapter 4). Comparison of the resources used in delivering a value driver with its importance provides an indication of whether it represents good value. The term 'cost/worth' is sometimes used to describe the ratio between the most economical method of satisfying a function and its proposed cost, and also acts as an indicator of whether it provides good value.

If the value driver is relatively unimportant but is shown to take a lot of resource to deliver, the MoV study team should consider alternative ways of achieving it. Resource saved in a selected area during this exercise can either be retained as a saving or applied where it will add more value.

5.4.2 Trading off

Often a project team faces a choice of whether to invest more money early in a project's life in order to save operating and/or maintenance costs. Discounted cash flow (DCF) analysis (see section 4.4.1.4) provides a method of estimating the period of time before the additional investment yields a positive return (referred to as the payback period). Many organizations have rules to forbid such additional investment if the payback period exceeds a prescribed time.

If the payback period is short, say three years or less, the impact of time on future cash flows is small, and undertaking DCF may not be necessary. It may be sufficient to divide the annual cash flow savings into the additional investment to assess the payback period.

Other examples of trading off include increasing resources to accelerate a project, building in features to reduce environmental impact or another identified risk factor, or incorporating features to improve productivity. In all cases, the ability to quantify improvements in value is required to justify any increase in the use of resources.

Example

A restaurant chain was reviewing its operations to reduce staffing costs. It commissioned a series of MoV studies to explore ways of improving productivity. Whole-life cost models were developed for each area of operations. These clearly showed that over the expected life of a restaurant, the net present value of staff costs exceeded 50% of the total, including refurbishment and maintenance costs. By investing a little more in equipment and improving working procedures, the chain was able to save in excess of 20% on the whole-life cost.

5.5   QUANTIFY VALUE

The value ratio, introduced in section 1.2, provides a means to assess value for money. Balancing the variable within the value ratio then provides a way to optimize value to the satisfaction of the key stakeholders and an organization's value priorities.

Whilst the use of resources can usually be measured reasonably easily (usually boiling down to some measure of cost), quantifying benefits – particularly the non-monetary ones – can be more difficult. A value-improving proposal should always include a quantitative analysis of how it improves value, both for benefits improvement and time and cost impact.

Individual value-improving proposals may be grouped together into scenarios to show the aggregate effect over a whole project.

5.5.1 Value index

Calculation of a value index provides one way to quantify monetary and non-monetary benefits alike over a whole project: how to do this is explained in Chapter 4. Having established the project value profile, the MoV study team can assess the current performance of the project against each value driver and develop a matrix. The value index provides a measure of how well the project, in its current state of development, satisfies the project objectives.

Whilst the value index demonstrates how well a project satisfies the requirements of a project (represented by value drivers), it does not provide any indication of whether the individual value drivers or the project as a whole represents value for money.

5.5.2 Value for money ratio

In a further refinement, the value index may be divided by the total estimated project cost to provide a value for money index. A project that has a very high value index may not provide best value for money if its costs are significantly higher than an alternative that provides slightly lower performance but at significantly less cost. The same comment can be made for projects arising from risk treatments. This refinement can be used when assessing different options at the early stages in a project. To monitor progress during the development of a project, the above exercise should be conducted at key project milestones and progress recorded.

The above method relies on achieving consensus across the main stakeholders in the programme or project and is therefore somewhat subjective. It does, however, provide a simple way to maximize value, taking account of non-monetary benefits.

The concept of the value for money ratio can be extended to programme and portfolio levels, where it will be critical for maximizing enterprise value.

5.6 MONITOR IMPROVEMENTS IN VALUE

All the activities described above may be wasted if the plan for implementing the value-improving proposals is not adequately monitored to ensure that expected improvements in value are actually realized.

An individual, who may be the study leader or a member of the project team, should be responsible for monitoring this task.

The most common method is for the regular project progress reports to include a summary log of the accepted value-improving proposals with a column indicating who is responsible for implementing them and a short statement on their status.

Alternatively, this process may be integrated with benefits realization management if that method is being used on the project.

5.7 LEARN LESSONS

At all stages of a programme or project, MoV will generate an audit trail of what decisions were made, why they were made, what worked well and added value, and what did not work so well and could be improved. All this information provides invaluable feedback to encourage continuous improvement, provided the information can be stored and made readily accessible to those who need it.

The learning from this store of information can be used in three ways:

- **To improve individual and team performance**
  It is good practice for the senior MoV practitioner and the study leaders to get together from time to time to review what they have been doing and share experiences. Regular meetings of this nature will help all those who are involved to learn from their peers and improve their individual performance in the future.

- **To feed back lessons across a programme of projects**
  If a project forms part of a programme of projects, there may be valuable lessons to be learned on one project that can be passed on to other projects. These may be communicated from one project to another within the programme by way of reports from the individual project MoV study leaders to the programme manager, probably through the project managers or executives.

- **To feed back lessons to the organization's internal projects**
  If the organization has a number of projects to which it wishes to apply MoV, lessons learned can be shared in a similar way to the examples above, by way of an accessible database and regular feedback meetings.

Environment: responding to external and internal influences

6

6 Environment: responding to external and internal influences

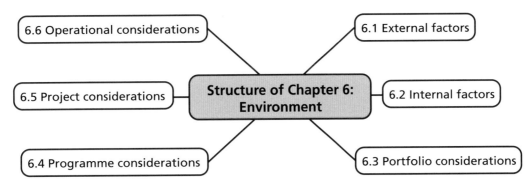

Figure 6.1 Structure of Chapter 6

Formulation of MoV policy, strategy and plans needs to take account of external and internal influences as well as the scale and complexity of the projects to which they are likely to be applied. This chapter describes some of the influences to which it should respond. These may influence both the perception of value and the form of the MoV activities.

Both external and internal factors will shape how organizations act, express desired outcomes and plan to achieve them (see Figure 6.2).

6.1 EXTERNAL FACTORS

All organizations should construct their business model in accordance with the external environment. The internal environment is shaped and influenced by it. Although this section touches on a wide range of issues, it should be read in relation to the approaches to implementation discussed in Chapter 5.

6.1.1 Political and legal influences

Political and legal influences arise from central and local government intervention as well as legal proceedings and case law. These comprise a huge range of subjects that will affect almost every activity undertaken.

Their influence will impact on perceptions of value as well as the need to adjust MoV plans to address the specific issues raised by these influences.

For example, emissions of carbon dioxide used to be regarded as an inevitable and unimportant consequence of doing business. Now, not only are unlimited emissions not permitted but they have a high value through the introduction of carbon emissions trading.

6.1.2 Environmental influences

Global climate change has kindled great interest in the so called 'triple bottom line' – 'people, planet and profit' is the descriptive phrase coined for Shell and widely used elsewhere. MoV addresses and enables reconciliation between the inherent conflicts in objectives combined in this measure by building consensus among stakeholders as to the best balance of benefits to be secured within available resources.

6.1.2.1 People

'People' refers to the social factors and to how the organization and its activities relate to the market, the community and its own employees. Maintenance of an organization's brand can have a significant impact on its success and it needs to be well communicated and maintained. 'People' also includes the cultural aspects such as the organization's perceived attitude towards demographics, employment, health and safety. Trends in social factors affect the demand for a company's products and how that company operates. Nowhere is this more apparent that in the issue of sustainability.

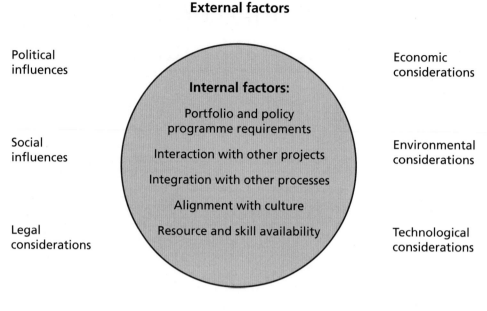

Figure 6.2 Interrelationship between internal and external environments

Some years ago, 'green supporters' used to be seen as a radical fringe group. Now everyone is keen to flaunt their green credentials. MoV provides transparency of value for its customers and ensures that their views are represented.

6.1.2.2 Planet

Organizations are becoming increasingly encouraged to minimize their use of unsustainable resources and cut pollution and waste. Nowhere is this more apparent than in the focus on carbon reduction. An organization's attitude and practice towards minimizing its impact on the planet's resources is now a major factor in enhancing the brand and will have significant influence on how it approaches projects. MoV policy will be shaped by the organization's attitudes to using resources more effectively and generating less waste, as these will translate to value drivers at portfolio, programme and project levels.

Example
The UK Government's programme for minimizing waste, WRAP ('waste and resources action programme'), uses the principles of MoV to identify and encourage active measures to recycle or re-use materials that were once thrown away.

6.1.2.3 Profit

Despite the pressures to invest in their people and minimize their impact on the planet, it is vital that businesses remain viable and sustainable organizations.

The emphasis that MoV places on reconciling conflicting requirements and balancing the use of resources provides a powerful way to enhance profitability and maintain economic sustainability, without sacrificing commitments to the people and the planet.

6.1.3 Technological influences

Changes in technology have always provided strong drivers for change. Responding to change effectively requires an innovative approach to how things are done. One of MoV's strengths is the ability to stimulate innovation by considering alternative ways to deliver functions.

Changes in technology may also have a profound impact on the perceptions of value. This is nowhere more apparent than in consumer ICT products, where yesterday's exciting breakthroughs become today's performance differentiators and tomorrow's basic requirements.[11]

11 Reference to the Kano Quality Model put forward by Dr Noriaki Kano of the Tokyo Rika University in the late 1970s.

Example

When mobile telephones were first introduced they were regarded as a status symbol for the high-flying business executive and commanded a very high price. As they became more widespread the price fell dramatically and they became available to the mass population. Attention turned to differentiating between telephones on quality, performance and appearance. Now, mobile telephones are an essential accessory for all ages and we wonder how we ever managed without them.

6.1.4 Interaction with other projects

Whenever an organization embarks on a new initiative, it must take into account what other organizations operating in the same space are doing. At portfolio level such considerations will shape the organizational strategy. At programme level the shape of the programme will be optimized to exploit opportunities arising and be constrained by the impacts from other organizations' programmes.

With its emphasis on broad stakeholder involvement, MoV can help shape portfolio strategy and programme and project plans.

6.2 INTERNAL FACTORS

Having analysed the external situation, the executive board will reach conclusions on which parts have most impact and will respond with an appropriate portfolio strategy. It will then consider how to implement this strategy in the most effective manner to minimize disruption and in a timely manner.

6.2.1 Portfolio and policy considerations

The portfolio strategy will dictate the programme plans, which in turn will define the project plans. The MoV policy should reflect requirements of the portfolio strategy. Similarly, the MoV programme and project plans should be tailored to suit the project plans. This will require that the organization's value profile is reflected in the programme and project value profiles, thus ensuring consistency in the perception of value and the manner in which it is optimized across all activities.

If MoV is applied to a single project, whether or not it forms part of a wider programme, one of the tasks of the MoV study leader, when setting up the MoV plans, will be to align these to the organization's portfolio and programme requirements.

6.2.2 Alignment with organizational culture

The policy expresses how the company should operate and why this is desirable. This in turn will influence the culture. We have seen earlier how it is desirable to effect changes in culture, as necessary, to encourage people to collaborate in efforts to maximize the value of outputs, rather than simply deliver a service.

The MoV implementation strategy must take existing culture into account, and if the culture is significantly out of step with the need to maximize value, adjust accordingly.

One of the most effective ways to encourage participants in MoV to actively contribute to the quest for improved value is to offer incentives. If MoV is being applied across a programme of projects, developing competition between MoV study teams is equally effective.

People need to be convinced, rather than compelled, to change. Introducing something new can help make change happen and it needs total commitment and ownership by senior management in order to maintain momentum. (See Chapter 7 for more on this.) The role of reward for people who are good role models for the new ways of doing things is significant and should be built into the implementation of MoV.

6.2.3 Interaction with other projects

The considerations expressed in section 6.2.1 above should ensure that individual MoV project plans are aligned with programme plans and the organization's portfolio strategy.

Application of MoV should be included at all levels as a series of planned activities. MoV should be integrated into programme and project activities rather than be seen as a bolt-on extra or afterthought.

When considering the implementation plan for value-improving proposals, study teams need to be made aware that what they are doing may impact other projects and act accordingly.

Within a portfolio of programmes or a programme of projects, MoV provides a method of prioritizing their importance so that if resources are stretched there may be a need to prioritize those projects to which MoV is applied (see sections 6.2.4 and 6.2.5).

6.2.4 Integration with other processes

If it is intended to embed MoV into an organization, it will be necessary to consider its integration with other processes that may have an impact on it or with which it may be combined.

One such process is the management of risk (M_o_R). There are many ways in which M_o_R is compatible with MoV and lends itself to integration. For example, opportunities identified by risk management may be fed into MoV and integrated with the value-improving proposals. When assessing whether to recommend the implementation of a value-improving proposal, the risks, or disadvantages, of so doing should be taken into account. When establishing the relative importance of value drivers or other attributes, sensitivity analysis should include consideration of the risks that assessments may be inaccurate.

The MoV senior practitioner should also be aware of other processes that may be being applied to improve aspects of an organization's activities. MoV could be wasted if it conflicts with or is carried on in parallel with other such activities.

6.2.5 Resource and skill availability

The planned MoV activities may be constrained by the availability of resources with the appropriate skills and knowledge to lead studies. Such constraints could result in a need to prioritize demand (so that MoV is applied in only those projects that have the highest potential for value improvement) or the need to hire in external resource with the appropriate competencies.

6.3 PORTFOLIO CONSIDERATIONS

All change activities needed to achieve an organization's strategic objectives are contained in its portfolio.

Therefore, every programme must relate back to and reflect the strategic intent of the portfolio.

6.4 PROGRAMME CONSIDERATIONS

6.4.1 Relation to other programmes

Implementation of an organization's vision is achieved by putting in place a portfolio of programmes or projects. Where a programme is one of several, it will be necessary to apply MoV at portfolio level to coordinate approaches and identify the benefits across all programmes. The information to permit this will derive from the outputs of programme- and project-level MoV activities reported upwards through the MoV board to the executive board.

Feedback from this exchange of information will inform the programme MoV plan.

Each formal MoV study and appropriate follow-up activities should be represented on the programme and project master schedules. To maximize effectiveness, MoV activities should be planned from the outset in the end-to-end programme and project schedules rather than added in later. It is possible, however, that some unplanned studies may be required to address unexpected situations or divergences from the project plans.

6.4.2 MoV programme plan

The initial MoV programme plan will be informed by the portfolio strategy and feedback from other programmes described above. It will also be influenced by the ongoing activities within the programme itself as the projects report progress to the programme manager and this information is transferred to the other projects.

Feedback from all studies will be used to improve performance on other projects within the programme, particularly for lessons learned, and where necessary escalated to the programme board to inform decision-making. The programme manager will, via the MoV plan and studies, agree what measures are necessary (see Figure 6.3).

6.5 PROJECT CONSIDERATIONS

Within the project, one of the main considerations of MoV activities is to enable projects to deliver optimized outputs to specified quality within time, cost and scope constraints. MoV should be applied at all stages of the project (see Figure 6.4) as described earlier in this guide.

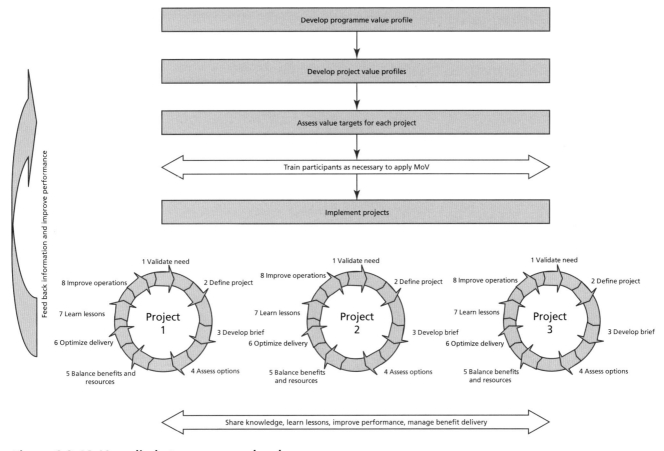

Figure 6.3 MoV applied at programme level

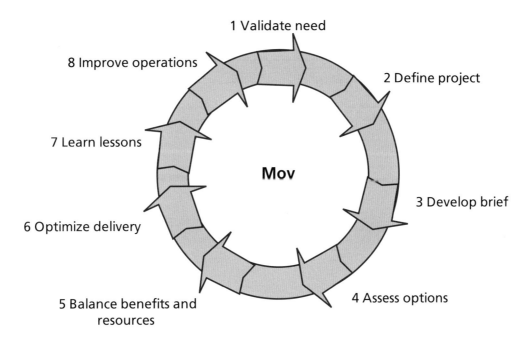

Figure 6.4 MoV applied at project level

The extent of MoV activity will include considerations of the project's scale, complexity and type. Regardless of scale, the underlying principles and processes of MoV should all be applied. Modifications may be made to depth and duration of these; for example, the duration of a formal study may be shorter for a simple project than would be necessary for a larger one.

Time should be allowed in the project schedule for MoV activities and, if required, for training for participants.

Where a project spans different organizations (a bidding consortium for example) it is vital that consensus is reached between the stakeholders as to the best way to balance the variables to maximize value.

6.5.1 Internal influences

The project board is influenced by the programme board and by the priority of the project. Depending on the business imperatives of the organization, it may emphasize one type of value driver (for example speed of delivery) over another (for example capital cost). This will be reflected in the value profile but may also put pressure on the time allowed for undertaking MoV studies. Careful judgement is needed to ensure adequate time is given for MoV work.

6.5.2 External impacts

In the case of a project whose effects will be visible outside the organization, consideration should be made of the wider community and any relevant legislation taken into account. This may require subject specialists or external stakeholders to be brought into the team. Care may be needed to maintain or enhance the organization's image or brand.

6.6   OPERATIONAL CONSIDERATIONS

There are two sets of circumstances in which operational MoV studies may be advantageous. Firstly, those ensuing once the project has delivered its output and been commissioned for use. In this case any MoV study will focus on improving and fine-tuning the operations under the new conditions. The second relates to improving existing service operations.

Both respond to internal and external influences by means of an operational improvement MoV study to align its operations with business objectives, which are themselves designed to respond to changing conditions.

6.6.1 Internal influences

Communication must be ensured between operational managers and those with strategic, programme and project responsibilities impacting the operation. An example could be where a project impacts several departments at once (for example, implementing an enterprise resource planning (ERP) system) as this will change the way in which people do things.

Both internal and external customers will be identified and their needs addressed in an operational improvement MoV study, although the needs of the end user must always be paramount. Without end users, any service is pointless and should be eliminated. Within this context, however, the internal customer has much valuable input to contribute to improving operations. Operational improvement studies are normally undertaken as recurring activities over a period of time. Each study may be considered as a separate project, subject to the same considerations as described elsewhere in this guide.

6.6.2 External impacts

Operational improvement MoV studies are normally commissioned to address a specific problem or area of low performance, or when circumstances have changed (for example, a change in the statutory duties to be performed by a local authority). They may be triggered from external survey reports indicating a need for improvement or change. They may also be brought on by the failure of another project to deliver all the expected benefits.

Whatever the circumstances, the MoV study leader should take account of the external influences and tailor the processes used, the stakeholders consulted and the members of the study team accordingly.

Embedding MoV into
an organization

7

7 Embedding MoV into an organization

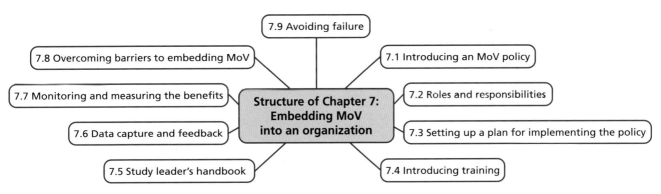

Figure 7.1 Structure of Chapter 7

Many organizations will wish to introduce MoV on a project-by-project basis – either to convince senior management of its effectiveness or because demand may not warrant setting up internal delivery capability. In these cases external resource may be procured on an 'as-needed' basis. Should the scale of MoV applications become large and frequent, thus justifying internal delivery capability, organizations should introduce and embed MoV in a manner that is consistent with their other processes so that it becomes a cost-effective part of the way in which they conduct business rather than something procured externally. This chapter describes a process for doing this. The degree to which these processes are implemented should be proportionate to the scale of MoV activities.

If organizations anticipate that their MoV needs will be minimal, they may prefer to adopt a less formal approach to that described below, sufficient for their people to understand the benefits of MoV without committing to building up a full internal delivery capability. When such organizations apply MoV to a programme or project they can procure qualified study leaders from third parties to deliver MoV.

Other organizations may already have people engaged on other work who wish to add MoV to their set of skills. For these, management structures will already be in place, and much of what follows will not be needed.

Regardless of the above, those who wish to become MoV study leaders should possess the level of knowledge contained in this guide and the facilitation skills necessary to deliver MoV effectively.

The processes described below describe a top-down approach to introducing MoV. Commonly, senior management will need to be convinced of the merits of fully embedding MoV before committing to the process. In such cases, demonstrating its effectiveness on a few trial projects is an excellent way to build confidence and tailor the method to suit the specific requirements of the organization.

It should be noted that although embedding MoV in the manner described here will require some investment, there is significant value to be gained form having an effective management structure in place to support competent study leaders. The main benefits include:

- Greater efficiency in the delivery of MoV and the benefits gained theretrom
- Continuous improvement in MoV delivery
- More effective use of internal resources by broadening their capabilities
- More cost-effective delivery than procuring external resource
- Better control over delivery and greater responsiveness
- Developing a value-conscious culture
- Known study leaders and better relationships with users.

For MoV to become fully embedded into an organization, it will need a consistent approach over a period of time as described in earlier chapters. In order to establish this environment, it will be necessary to formally introduce the discipline, including the steps described below (see also Figure 7.2):

- Introducing the MoV policy
- Establishing suitable roles and responsibilities
- Setting up a strategy for implementing the policy
- Introducing training
- Providing guidance on how MoV will be used on projects
- Developing procedures for data capture, feedback
- Monitoring and measuring the benefits achieved
- Overcoming barriers to embedding MoV.

In common with many management activities, an enthusiastic and supportive culture should be encouraged within the organization, starting at the top and continuing through all levels of management and staff. Experience has shown that such support will not develop and cannot be sustained without a planned series of activities to introduce, build upon and maintain the MoV principles described in outline in Chapter 2. This chapter describes how to introduce measures that will lead to the establishment of a sustainable culture along with mechanisms for delivering the benefits of MoV.

It also addresses how to overcome some of the barriers to the adoption of MoV and the consequences of not implementing positive measures for improving value.

Sometimes senior management have to be convinced of the need to introduce MoV, in which case it may be appropriate to trial its introduction on a few projects and use the successful outcomes of MoV to support the argument for wider introduction. When adopting this approach it is still necessary to have some visible senior management support and accountability to encourage take-up by managers.

7.1 INTRODUCING AN MoV POLICY

The policy is the first clear statement of support by senior management and, as such, should communicate how MoV will be implemented throughout the organization to help achieve its strategic objectives. The policy will also describe why it is needed and outline what it is.

7.1.1 Composition

The MoV policy will contain:

- Reasons for adopting MoV and how it contributes to corporate objectives

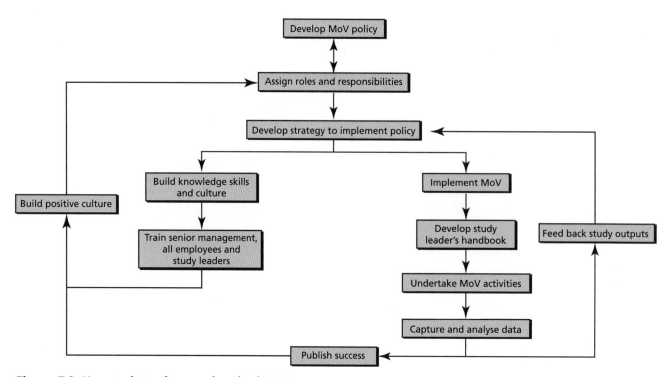

Figure 7.2 How to introduce and embed MoV

- A high-level outline description of the key MoV processes, why they are used and signposts to other MoV processes
- Statement of who is the explicit policy owner and other key roles and responsibilities
- Responsibilities of all other participants and their expected contributions
- Policy on training
- Clear terminology for describing events and key roles in order to promote a common language
- Guidelines on how to measure the benefits arising from MoV
- Principles of capturing data and learning from experience for continuous improvement
- Statements on how the reward system will respond to positive and negative MoV performance
- Guidelines on setting appropriate targets for improving value
- Guidelines on when and how MoV studies are to be conducted
- Reporting requirements
- Explanation of how MoV relates to other policies in use in the organization
- Sign-off by the board.

Taking each of these points in turn:

- **Reasons for adopting MoV** No matter how MoV is introduced, it should be aligned with the organization's overall goals and with other policies and complementary processes in use in the organization. Some existing processes may need adapting to accommodate and encourage the use of MoV. In addition, it should be noted that:
  - Goals vary hugely depending on what the organization is set up to do. Most government organizations are set up to implement government policies through the procurement and/or delivery of public services in a manner that provides the greatest benefits to society and efficient use of public funds. Private organizations, on the other hand, are generally set up to generate wealth. In neither sector is success in achieving these goals assured. The use of MoV along with other Best Management Practice guides will improve the chances or make it easier for organizations to achieve success.
  - The value profile of a public organization will, for the reasons outlined above, differ significantly from that of the private sector.

Other organizations such as charities will also have their distinctive value profiles.
  - All organizations are different. When setting up the MoV policy it is therefore essential to establish the organization's value profile so that all involved can understand it and contribute to its achievement.
- **Description of processes** The policy should set out the core processes to be used in MoV applications in differing circumstances. This will discourage study leaders from taking short cuts and thus undermining the quality of the method. It will also reduce the incidence of a tick-box culture. Undertaking a health check (see Appendix C) from time to time will verify whether MoV is being applied rigorously.
- **The MoV policy owner** is likely to be the sponsor who represents MoV on the executive board. The key roles and responsibilities will be those outlined in section 7.2.
- **Roles and responsibilities** These are described in section 7.2 and should be set out in the strategy. Senior management must take every opportunity to promote MoV strongly and enthusiastically so that the rest of the organization appreciates its contribution to improving performance.
- **Training** A critical decision in developing MoV policy is whether or not to rely on third parties to deliver MoV, in whole or in part, or to train up and develop internal resource. This decision may be influenced by several factors – for example, the size of the organization, the frequency of application of MoV, broader organizational policy to restrict activities to core business, the nature of the projects to which MoV will be applied, and the existing or anticipated skills profile in the organization. Even if it is decided to employ external resource to deliver MoV, it will still be necessary to provide training to employees in order that they can understand, initiate, oversee and contribute to MoV studies.
- **Terminology** The policy should use terms that are common throughout the organization and specific to MoV. Please refer to the glossary for suggestions on standard terminology.
- **Measuring benefits** MoV will result in both monetary and non-monetary benefits. Whilst monetary benefits are relatively easy to measure objectively, non-monetary benefits might require a more subjective means of

assessment. Therefore, the metrics for assessing them must be selected with care, especially as they may be indirect.

> **Example**
>
> An MoV study to improve the operational efficiency of the outpatient's department in a hospital needed a metric to assess customer satisfaction. After some deliberation they chose to measure the number of letters of complaint received. Records made before the improvement project was implemented provided a baseline against which to measure future improvements.

- **Capturing data and learning from experience** If the organization is to learn from experience and improve MoV performance, it will be necessary to capture, analyse and disseminate outputs from MoV studies. The policy should set out who is responsible for doing this and how the information should be used.
- **Reward system** A strong motivator for encouraging employees to support and use MoV is to link success with the reward system. Such links must be carefully thought through to avoid abuse or inadvertently rewarding the wrong behaviours.
- **Setting targets** Targets and improvements in value sought by different organizations will vary depending on the organization's goals. For example, whilst maintaining a healthy financial situation will always be important, an organization in the health sector will place greater emphasis on improving the health of its customers and set targets accordingly. The policy should provide guidance on these priorities.
- **When and how to conduct MoV studies** The level of appropriate MoV effort should reflect the size, complexity and importance of the project to which it is applied. Some small projects may not warrant any MoV study. A small project that is repeated many times within a wider programme, however, may warrant a greater degree of effort, since the benefits arising from it will be multiplied many times over the whole programme. Major projects, particularly those contributing to a wider programme, will warrant significant effort. The policy should give guidance on the level of MoV effort to be applied in different circumstances.

- **Reporting requirements** In order that the senior MoV practitioner and the SRO may gauge the success of MoV and take appropriate action to maintain and improve it, the policy should set out who should receive reports and the level of detail that these should contain.
- **Relationship with other policies** The MoV policy should complement other policies rather than duplicate or conflict with them. This is essential if MoV is to become embedded into the way in which the organization operates.
- **Sign-off by the board** The MoV policy will be one of the obligatory documents in the organization and therefore needs to be formally signed off by the board under the same process as applies to other documents of similar status. Periodic updates to the policy should be signed off similarly.

7.1.2 Multiple policies

Sometimes an organization may have several significantly different strands of activity. In such cases, there may need to be variants on the MoV policy in order to reflect these different activities. Where this is the case, it is important that each variant clearly states the reasons for its implementation and to what it applies.

7.2 ROLES AND RESPONSIBILITIES

The implementation of MoV to maximize value for an organization is regarded as good practice and, as such, should not be discretionary once adopted. It is nevertheless vital that clear roles and responsibilities are assigned if it is to be successful.

A suggested management structure is illustrated in Figure 7.3.

The representative to the executive board should:

- Have a good understanding of (but not necessarily be an expert on) MoV
- Share a good relationship with the board so that issues relating to MoV can be raised as they occur
- Attend board meetings from time to time
- Chair the MoV steering group (or MoV board)
- Be likely to have other responsibilities in the organization in addition to MoV duties

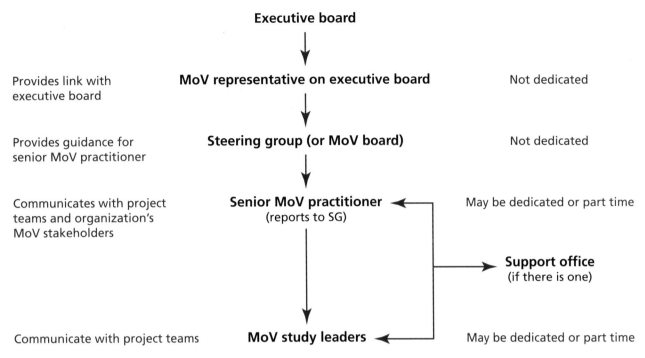

Figure 7.3 A suggested MoV management structure

- Encourage the use of MoV and the building of a culture at board level that motivates all involved to seek to maximize value in all their activities, through the use of incentives or otherwise.

The senior MoV practitioner will be actively engaged in all aspects of the MoV programme and must demonstrate leadership and competence in the subject to inspire and motivate all those who are involved. Depending on the volume of MoV activity in the organization, the role may or may not be full time. The senior MoV practitioner should:

- Be experienced in MoV
- Have both the knowledge and skill to apply it
- Report to the steering group (if it exists)
- Be responsible for implementing the MoV policy and contribute to its development and updating from time to time.

Study leaders may be drawn from any part of the organization and will be selected on the grounds of their knowledge and skill in applying MoV processes. In addition to a thorough knowledge of MoV, good study leaders will need all or some of the following skills and characteristics:

- Positive attitude
- Self starter
- Inquisitive nature

- Excellent facilitator and communicator
- Good leader
- Generosity – to give credit to others
- Low sensitivity to criticism
- Confidence in success.

Some of these characteristics may be acquired through training but others will form part of an individual's character. Study leaders should be selected with these characteristics in mind.

The selection of the appropriate people in the roles of senior MoV practitioner and study leaders will have a positive impact on developing a value-conscious culture.

The key roles referred to above are summarized in Table 7.1.

Depending on the scale of MoV activity, no extra headcount may be required for MoV adoption. Most of the role descriptions here can be provided by refocusing existing roles – MoV should be regarded as a new way of working rather than an additional workload. The titles given are purely for ease of explanation and may be appropriate only in larger organizations.

Table 7.1 Key roles

Level	Activity	Purpose	Done by	Training needs
Organization	**Full alignment of MoV activities with organizational objectives**	Set the business objectives and ensure MoV is in step.	**Executive board** This term is used to denote the most senior decision-making body in an organization. It may be one person, or several.	Some awareness training would be helpful to ensure understanding of the MoV sponsor below.
	Promote MoV	Ensure value is the first consideration in all decision-making. Agree relevant feedback mechanisms and ensure adequate resource.	There should be a **representative at board level**. In smaller organizations, this may be the CEO; in larger ones, another director.	Needs to be convinced of MoV benefits, whether through awareness training or experience.
	Oversee MoV implementation	Ensure full alignment of individual MoV activities with organization objectives.	An **MoV board or steering group** is helpful where MoV implementation is likely to be large in scale, involving many programmes and projects.	This is an optional role, depending on appropriateness. Awareness training is advisable where taken up.
	Import MoV skills and knowledge	Ensure MoV activities are effective.	The **senior MoV practitioner** is a role that requires skills and knowledge that are unlikely to already exist in the organization. Where the scale of implementation is small, this could be provided by an external resource or combined with another role of a similar nature.	Full qualification and experience is needed. A full-time, dedicated resource would be needed, at least in the short term, for full implementation in a larger organization.
	Provide data for use in studies and communicate results and learning	Track performance improvements in line with agreed value priorities.	Some organizations have a **support office** that can support MoV activities either within the organization or during application on programmes or projects.	No MoV training needed, but awareness training may be helpful. This is likely only to be available in larger concerns and is not essential.

Level	Activity	Purpose	Done by	Training needs
Application	Lead MoV studies	Lead and facilitate a suite of studies to achieve a given objective in accordance with the implementation plan.	**Study leaders** are competent MoV practitioners responsible for all aspects of planning, implementing and reporting on MoV studies.	Full training is necessary for in-house study leaders. External practitioners can be procured if a pilot study is preferred.
	Participate in studies	Contribute to studies and developing proposals, and see these through from executive board presentation to implementation.	Members of the **MoV study team** should be drawn from all key stakeholder groups involved in advising on and delivering the programme or project, and/or may be affected by its outcome.	Members of the study team may require awareness training.

7.3 SETTING UP A PLAN FOR IMPLEMENTING THE POLICY

The MoV policy implementation strategy will be written by the senior MoV practitioner and signed off by the steering group.

It should set out clearly how the activities required by the policy should be implemented. These will include the following:

- A summary of the requirements of the policy so that all participants in MoV are aware of it
- The level of training and qualifications required, by whom, and where and how these can be acquired
- An outline of the key objectives of MoV in the organization, and guidelines on selecting projects to which MoV will be applied
- A high-level outline of the key MoV processes, why they are used and signposts to more detailed sources of information (including this guide)
- How MoV will be applied to projects (see study leader's handbook in section 7.5), including scaling the level of effort to suit the size and complexity of the project
- Roles and responsibilities of all participants, including those who will contribute to but not lead MoV studies, and the project support office (if one exists) in providing support generally
- Reporting requirements and how to capture data for analysis and learning lessons.

The plan should be made available to all those who are involved in MoV activities within the organization.

The plan may propose that MoV be introduced on a few projects initially to demonstrate success and facilitate fine-tuning of the study leader's handbook (see section 7.5).

7.4 INTRODUCING TRAINING

A good understanding of MoV is necessary to instil its principles and embed a systematic approach. Unless firmly embedded, there is a risk that future changes in leadership may undo progress made to date. The cost of training will be more than recouped by the improvements in value resulting from the successful implementation of MoV. Many of these improvements will not be forthcoming without MoV.

> **Example**
>
> A consumer goods manufacturer wanted to adopt MoV to improve the return on its investments in manufacturing facilities. It employed a firm of external MoV practitioners to train a group of potential MoV study leaders to MoV practitioner level. These trainees then applied their new skills under the supervision of the experienced external practitioners until they gained the confidence and competence to practise unassisted. The MoV programme contributed to an improvement in return on investment of more than 10%.

It is unnecessary to train everyone to the same level, as they will not all be involved to the same extent.

Training may be applied at four levels:

■ Awareness training for individuals who simply need to know what MoV is so that they can interact with their colleagues. This may be aimed at different levels of employee, from senior managers to more junior staff, since each will need a different level of understanding.
■ Foundation-level training for those who are likely to participate in MoV activities.
■ Practitioner-level training for those who will be actively involved with and contribute to MoV studies. Individuals who wish to lead studies may require additional training in such skills as facilitation.
■ Training to advanced study leader level involving skills and knowledge for those who intend to deliver MoV services.

Sometimes, when implementing an MoV study, it is necessary to provide 'just-in-time' training to participants to help them contribute fully to the study (see Figure 5.2). This is similar to awareness training (as described in the first point above) and would normally be provided by the study leader.

Training at awareness level may be undertaken by internal staff who have an understanding of the principles and practice of MoV. It could also be provided by e-learning or through involvement in MoV studies on projects.

Mentoring by experienced MoV practitioners is an excellent way for novices to improve their proficiency. The best way to learn and gain experience is, however, by applying MoV to live projects, possibly under the guidance of a mentor initially.

Training at other levels should be delivered by accredited trainers using accredited material. This guide provides the basis of the Best Management Practice MoV qualifications, which are part of the PPM suite of qualifications. Other qualifications are available through professional institutions internationally.[12]

All training should contribute to raising both the organizational and individual levels of maturity on learning generally and MoV in particular. In Appendix D, organizational maturity and individual competency models, consistent with the Portfolio, Programme and Project Management Maturity Model (P3M3), are discussed.

7.5 STUDY LEADER'S HANDBOOK

A key document that the senior MoV practitioner should produce describes how to apply MoV to projects and programmes. This document effectively forms the study leader's handbook on how to use their accumulated knowledge to develop and implement a project-specific MoV plan. It is the culmination of all the effort set out in the previous four sections of this chapter. It should broadly describe the MoV project plan illustrated in Figure 5.2.

The study leader's handbook should set out the following:

■ Guidance on selecting on which projects to apply MoV and the level of effort to be applied commensurate with their size, complexity and importance.
■ How to identify the key stakeholders in the project and define the objectives of the study.
■ How to select the required processes and the level of effort needed to achieve the study objectives.
■ How to select the study participants and gauge whether or not they need training.
■ Where and how to gather information, including what information may be needed.
■ How to use the information that has been gathered to provide useful input to the MoV study and share this with the participants.
■ How to conduct the study, run workshops, generate value-improving proposals, obtain decisions from the project management teams, agree implementation plans, report the outputs and follow up.
■ How to capture data and use it to learn lessons and provide feedback for continuous improvement.

---

12 For example: the Institute of Value Management (UK) at www.ivm.org.uk; Society of American Value Engineers, http://value-eng. org; and Institute of Value Management Australia, www.value-management.com.au

The project plan should spell out the role of project support office in providing technical support as well as capturing and disseminating the records accumulated during t e MoV programme. Without access to this information, future projects risk wasting much time and money, so it is essential to consider how individuals can retrieve this data.

7.6 DATA CAPTURE AND FEEDBACK

Data capture is essential to a learning organization and culture. All study output has worth in terms of supporting decisions made and lessons learned from those decisions. Consideration is needed to determine how lessons learned on one project can be transferred to another, whether in the same programme or not.

Similarly, whilst the policy and implementation guide will have been developed with a view to optimizing the application of MoV, feedback from MoV studies will provide valuable information on what worked well in practice and what was less successful. This provides the basis for building on successful processes and improving those which could benefit from some help.

Responsibility for ensuring retained data is captured, analysed and accessible for sharing with others may rest with the senior MoV practitioner or may be undertaken by the project support office, where this exists.

Thought is needed to determine what is to be captured, how long it is to be kept, the media in which it is kept and, above all, the way in which it is to be shared. The structure, location, form and permission levels of these records will determine how they are accessed and by whom. Enabling ready access to those who need it is one of the most difficult aspects of setting up a knowledge database. A framework should be established for storing the data, providing 'labels', such as key words, project type and sector, and so on to facilitate search and retrieval. Lessons learned, especially if they are negative, are often lost to future projects and this wastes time and money reinventing the wheel. Capturing, recording and maintaining a good knowledge database requires skill and resource. This role is ideally suited to a good support office, if available.

Contributions to and use of the knowledge database should be mandatory.

The best source of MoV data is the reports that are produced giving the outputs from each study. This reinforces the need for these reports to be comprehensive and accurate.

Typically the following information may be gathered:

- Value-improving proposals (whether implemented or not)
- Classification of the project type, context (e.g. whether part of a programme or not) and objectives
- The agreed study outputs and implementation plan
- The success or otherwise of achieving the expected increases in value.

This information may then be analysed to provide the following easily accessible outputs:

- A record of all studies undertaken, their classification, dates, outputs (initial and final) and feedback
- Information on the most common and effective value-improving measures for different project types
- Performance trends to inform senior management about the effectiveness of MoV
- Case studies or success stories for sharing and/ or publication
- Information for future project audits
- What should be done differently next time.

7.6.1 MoV study records

A readily accessible and detailed record of all MoV studies undertaken will save considerable time in reviewing past experience. This information may be used in marketing, learning from others with similar experience and providing precedent for similar projects.

7.6.2 Effective value-improving measures

Information on the most common and effective value-improving measures provides invaluable input for conducting similar studies and a firm foundation for project teams to build on from the outset.

7.6.3 Trends

Senior management and others will want to understand trends in the outcomes of MoV studies and programmes. Performance trends (for example plotting the added value realized by project type over time) will help senior management focus their MoV efforts where they are most effective and avoid wasting resources. Benefits, both monetary and non-monetary, should be recorded centrally to show trends in the effectiveness of the programme and the cost benefit ratio for MoV.

Suitable key performance indicators for MoV fall into two types.

- Embedding measures:
  - Proportion of projects or programmes to which MoV is regularly applied
  - Numbers of formal studies undertaken

  Monitoring such statistics allows the rate of take-up to be measured and future resource requirements, such as training, to be estimated.
- Outcome measures:
  - Cost savings compared with total costs of applying MoV
  - Types of projects to which MoV is applied and the relative success of such applications.

Trend information will enable the senior MoV practitioner and senior management to identify where MoV is working well, where performance needs to be improved and demonstrate that those projects employing effective MoV deliver added value.

7.6.4 Case studies

Publicizing success stories is the best way to secure senior management commitment and win new followers. By keeping MoV achievements in view as much as possible, corporate memory will be protected from changes in senior management and other project-related resource.

Similarly, there is no better way to demonstrate the effectiveness of MoV and to build a supportive culture throughout an organization than by sharing positive outcomes. Success breeds success and such case studies should form a core part of any training exercise.

Not only does this encourage senior management support, but it instils a sense of pride in those who contributed. This sense of personal ownership of a successful result is a powerful motivator in repeating that performance. In addition, such individuals generally acquire a good deal of kudos, which can improve career opportunities; it is important to consider how to retain these people in the organization.

Over time, it should be possible to build up a significant library of cases. These could be used to enhance the reputation of an organization that can demonstrate a successful track record of maximizing value in all its transactions.

The precise components of a good case study will vary, just as organizations do, but all will have certain features in common:

- An abstract searchable by key words, which makes the case study easier to find
- An indication of the challenges faced, why a change was necessary and what the project was seeking to achieve
- An outline of the methodology of moving from the original state to the new state, to reflect the key challenges and strategies used to overcome them
- A description of specific changes made and how and why they were selected
- A statement of the benefits delivered. Since these will vary over time, they will need to be updated periodically and the period defined. Where impacts are non-monetary, a means by which they can be measured must be described and the results given.

Although there is a lot of information here, case studies should be quite concise, which will encourage people to read them.

7.6.5 Audit trail

Many projects take several years to complete. Throughout that time they are likely to see changes in management personnel as well as the business environment. To provide an understanding of why certain decisions were taken, records should provide a clear explanation of the material on which the study was based and the MoV analysis resulting in the course of action agreed by the team.

7.6.6 Feedback for improving performance

While all MoV procedures should be rigorously applied, organizations should be prepared to adapt and amend them, within the bounds of this guide, to build on those things that work well and change or improve delivery of those that are less successful. The needs of all organizations differ. It is important to adapt procedures to suit the circumstances in which they are used and ways in which the organization operates.

If MoV is taken to heart by the whole organization, then performance will drive motivation up and a virtuous circle will result. Individuals can improve how they do things and share their successes with others; they will understand what the priorities of the organization are because these are described simply and clearly in the MoV plan; they can remedy any gaps in their knowledge or skill sets in relation to these objectives with help from the organization; they will learn from their mistakes and must be allowed to do so; and they will ask questions and need to know this is acceptable. All these things contribute to the culture of a learning organization and a personally rewarding existence that benefits the organization and those whom it serves (see Figure 7.4).

To apply the procedures as if they were set in stone and by rote will have an adverse effect. There is a risk that MoV could become a tick-box procedure – for example, to get approval to fund a project that might not offer any benefit to anyone, or might fall short of its potential to add real value. Such a culture is likely to discourage involvement and improvement in MoV and should be avoided by clearly demonstrating the benefits delivered.

7.7 MONITORING AND MEASURING THE BENEFITS

All projects are planned on the basis of providing benefits to the stakeholders. One of the primary purposes of MoV is to enhance the expected benefits to add more value.

The main outcomes from a successful MoV study or series of studies will include the following benefits:

- Enhanced satisfaction of the needs of the various stakeholders, both monetary and non-monetary

- More effective use of resources including money, time, manpower and materials
- Enhanced relationships between the participants leading to increased performance.

In order that these value enhancements may be realized, it will be necessary to undertake the following activities:

- Record the expected additional benefits (for example, by way of the MoV study report. If a benefits register exists, this may be incorporated in the study report.
- Provide the means to measure both monetary and non-monetary value improvements.
- Monitor the implementation of the value-improving proposals that are included in the agreed implementation plan.
- Take such actions as may be needed to prevent loss of (or further enhance) the expected improvements in value.
- On project completion, record the enhancements actually achieved and compare this with expectations.
- Provide feedback for improving future MoV performance.

In many organizations, these activities will be undertaken by the project teams in their regular project reviews, with or without input from the MoV study leader. They may also be undertaken by the project support office.

Many projects include a benefits realization process. In such cases the enhanced benefits arising from MoV studies may be introduced as a project change and managed as part of that process. If MoV enhancements to benefits are to be managed in this way, the value-improving proposals should include the information required in the benefits profile.

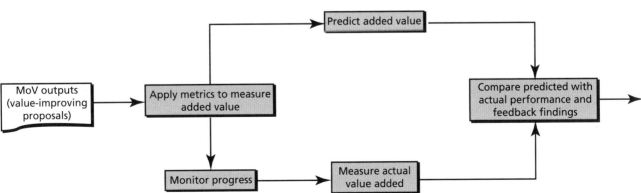

Figure 7.4 Feedback for improving performance

Monitoring the implementation of value-improving proposals at project reviews provides a reliable way to ensure their delivery.

Whatever method is adopted, failure to manage the implementation plan to secure the benefits will result in a reduction or loss of the added value provided by MoV.

7.8 OVERCOMING BARRIERS TO EMBEDDING MoV

This section explores some of the barriers that may be encountered when embedding MoV and suggests ways in which to overcome them. Some of the most common barriers are listed below:

- The belief that there are already processes for maximizing value and that project teams should be using these intuitively throughout the project. 'We do it anyway.'
- The belief that applying MoV processes rigorously takes up too much time and is a waste of resource, particularly where time is short. 'It takes too much time.'
- The belief that competitive fee bidding resulting in a tight fixed fee will discourage designers from accepting re-work due to changes, even if these result in enhanced value. 'We can't afford to make the changes.'
- A culture that does not encourage maximizing value if it involves additional unrewarded effort: inappropriate incentives and lack of accountability. 'What's in it for me?'
- A reluctance to change working practices which are already embedded. 'Don't fix it if it ain't broke.'
- Paying a fixed return on capital investment is unlikely to encourage value for money.

Below are some answers to these objections.

7.8.1 We do it anyway

A common cause for not implementing formal processes to maximize value is a belief that project teams should do this intuitively, or over-confidence that their intuition is right. In an ideal world, maybe this could be the case; however, the real world is becoming more and more competitive. To succeed in winning work, consultants and contractors will price what is requested in the bid documentation and no more. They will not price for expending effort

in improving the value of a project unless it is to their advantage. This requires a cultural shift from lowest cost to value for money or affordable cost.

MoV requires resource to implement and that costs money although, as demonstrated by statistics in the USA (see section 1.4.1), the benefits of applying MoV effectively and at the right time far outweigh its cost. Furthermore, embedding MoV in an organization together with some rationalization of processes should enable it not only to be applied without increasing headcount, but applied using existing resources more effectively.

Unless formal MoV is specified in accordance with best management practice (such as is set out in this guide), organizations are unlikely to receive a rigorous service and therefore to reap the full benefits of their investment. To counter this tendency, the requirement to apply MoV should be incorporated in tender documentation together with a requirement to demonstrate experience and provide a commitment to apply it in accordance with the tender requirements.

7.8.2 It takes too much time

In common with any management technique, assigning too little time and/or resource to implementing MoV significantly reduces its benefits. Scaling the level of effort to the size and complexity of a project should not be regarded as a licence to take short cuts.

The consequences of suboptimal or non-existent delivery of MoV include:

- Unnecessary costs generated by projects that do not have a robust business case for their existence
- Increased waste of materials or other scarce resources
- Poor performance of the completed project through a lack of clear understanding of the objectives
- Failure to achieve essential targets in sustainability or other corporate standards.

In short, a failure to provide value for money (as specifically required by UK government guidance, which is mandatory for public sector activities) would result.

Taking short cuts may be avoided by embedding the procedures described earlier in this chapter.

The added value from successful MoV studies generally far outweighs the costs arising from any delay. By careful management, the changes required to realize increased benefits should not cause delay. Indeed, any delay should be offset by reduced re-work from getting it right first time.

MoV activities should be programmed into the project from the outset, and contracts with the project team should include a requirement to participate and contribute to them.

7.8.3 We can't afford to make changes

Competitive fee bidding should include appropriate allowance for refining designs to optimize value, regardless of whether MoV is applied or not. If MoV is integrated into an organization's way of working, this should not be an issue: however, it may be undermined by inappropriate procurement practices.

It is good practice, when placing contracts, to build in an appropriate mechanism for incorporating changes arising from MoV studies.

If an MoV study results in outcomes that significantly enhance value, consideration should be given to sharing the rewards arising from making the changes with the project team. Generally, this reward amounts to a small fraction of the additional benefit and represents money well spent. Incentives may take several forms and, ideally, should result in benefits for client and contractors alike.

In the USA it is common practice to introduce value engineering change proposals (VECPs) into contracts. These incentivize contractors to introduce value-improving proposals that benefit all parties.

> **Example**
>
> The US Navy introduced an incentivizing VECP into the term contract for maintaining its bases. The VECP set out expectations of significant year-on-year cost reductions and reliability improvements backed by a contractor warranty that reliability would be upheld. In return they undertook not to re-tender the contract so long as the terms of the VECP were achieved.

7.8.4 What's in it for me?

Incentives need to be set very carefully. There are numerous examples of people taking advantage of incentives that have been poorly thought through or executed with the result that they gain the reward without having delivered the value.

The use of short-term incentives can encourage reckless risk-taking rather than establishing long-term benefit. Such behaviour can result in catastrophic loss of value when favourable conditions cease.

Appointing consultants or contractors on terms that increase their reward for increases in project costs or time is a recipe for inviting cost and time overruns and should be avoided. In such cases there will be huge resistance to implementing MoV.

Similarly, appointments based on lowest cost rather than best value can result in poor performance.

Any incentive payment mechanism must be used to reward 'good' behaviour. Pain/gain schemes allow the rewards to the project team to be aligned with the delivery of good value.

Often the culture in a large organization works against individuals making additional effort to improve value. They will receive their salary regardless, provided they work in accordance with their contract.

In such cases, senior management should consider introducing incentives for individuals to actively seek to enhance value and contribute to MoV studies. Such incentives should be designed to encourage long-term value enhancement rather than short-term gain (which might evaporate over the course of a long project).

Setting target incentives does not always result in the desired behaviour; however, changing culture can do so.

If management are not fully accountable for the activities over which they preside, they may not enforce the rigour needed to make MoV effective.

7.8.5 Don't fix it if it ain't broke

Many projects and services have been delivered successfully using traditional approaches that have not changed for many years. Unfortunately, in these times of rapid change, such established practices may not maximize value.

For many, there is a natural resistance to embracing changes in working practices when the existing ways of doing things seem to work adequately or if people have had insufficient time to assimilate the new processes.

In such cases it will be necessary to convince existing staff of the potential benefits to them and their organization. This may be achieved through training and the sharing of success stories.

7.8.6 Fixed returns on capital investment

If rewards are simply related to the amount of money spent, there is no incentive to maximize customer satisfaction or value for money. Reward should be based on the benefits delivered to customers.

7.9 AVOIDING FAILURE

In addition to the examples described above, the OGC published a report, agreed with the National Audit Office, entitled *The Common Causes of Project Failure*. In this, they specified eight common causes. MoV addresses all of these, directly or indirectly, as outlined in Table 7.2.

Table 7.2 Eight common causes of project failure

Cause	MoV response
Lack of clear links between the project and the organization's key strategic priorities, including agreed measures of success	This is clearly remedied by use of MoV which requires articulation of such links and clear project definition
Lack of clear senior management and ministerial ownership accountability and leadership	MoV itself cannot be implemented without senior management support and leadership. Ministers will tend to support success stories which MoV can provide. While senior management support is essential, MoV actually puts ownership of the improvements in value with the team
Lack of effective engagement with stakeholders	Engagement with stakeholders is a key principle of MoV, so the likelihood of its occurrence is significantly reduced through its use
Lack of skills and proven approach to project management and risk management	MoV training will help in terms of approach to project management, together with M_o_R or similar risk training
Too little attention to breaking development and implementation into manageable steps	MoV explores alternative ways of delivering benefits and can therefore contribute to optimizing the 'chunking' of development and implementation
Evaluation of proposals driven by initial price rather than long-term value for money (especially securing delivery of business benefits)	This is the reason why MoV uses whole-life costs as far as possible, as a better reflection of benefits gained. Changes in procurement policies and culture would help to address this cause
Lack of understanding of, and contact with, the supply industry at senior levels in the organization	MoV involves all links in the delivery process, as they are deemed to be stakeholders in their own right
Lack of effective project team integration between clients, the supplier team and the supply chain	MoV involves all links in the delivery process, as they are deemed to be stakeholders in their own right

Appendix A:
Document checklists

Appendix A: Document checklists

The following checklists are given alphabetically for ease of reference.

A.1   BRIEFING MEETING AGENDA

The objectives of a briefing meeting are to understand the project, the type of study that is needed, study logistics and how any feedback arrangements will be handled. The study leader should raise questions to meet each of these. As a guide, the following will normally give most of the right information, but should always be tailored to need.

About the project or programme:

- What will it do? Define the scope.
- What are the objectives?
- What improvements would you expect to see? What specific measures and targets are there?
- What is the structure of the organization being affected? Who are the stakeholders?
- Are there any specific issues that need to be addressed?
- When must the study deliver?
- What data needs to be shared by the study team?
- What point in the project lifecycle has been reached?
- What value drivers or primary functions are relevant? Value drivers are integral to successful delivery.
- What basis should be used for whole-life costing and over what period will it be applied?

About this particular study:

- What are the objectives for the study? What is in scope?
- Are there any givens that should not be challenged? Are there any specific issues that should be discussed?
- How will you judge if the study was a success?
- Where can the data needed by the study team be found?
- How should the data be analysed and later presented?
- Is it possible to fix a date for presenting results?

- To whom and how often should the study report be made?

Considerations for study working:

- Who are the recommended team members? Do they know each other? Are all necessary skills/disciplines represented?
- How should the study be structured?
- Where should it be held? What facilities are needed?
- How should team members communicate with each other?
- Who will manage the communications process?

Development work and feedback mechanisms:

- How will progress be monitored and reported?
- Can measures used in initial evaluation be adapted to form measurable targets? How will these be monitored?
- How often should project reviews occur? Who will lead these reviews?

A.2   COMMUNICATIONS CHECKLIST

Reference to the 'Five Ws and an H' method provides a good checklist for any communication. The important points are to visualize the exact circumstances in which the information is to be received. This will then suggest the best way to receive it: for example, should it be heard by everyone at the same time in order to avoid later distortion through other people, or is it sensitive and best shared with a small group or transmitted individually? Consider what you want to happen next and how you will determine whether it does happen.

It is also helpful to reward good communication and also to promote a two-way communication flow as much as possible, in order to generate involvement. Remember to audit communication success and encourage experimentation as far as possible, rewarding activities that worked.

Key questions are:

- Why are you communicating?
- Who is the target audience?

- Who will deliver the message?
- What are you trying to say? Can you explain the essence of it in two lines or fewer? (If you cannot do this, it is likely that others will find it difficult.)
- When are you going to tell people? Timing can be crucial in change processes.
- How much information will you give?
- How is the message to be conveyed?
- How accurate and presentable is the information? If any data measures were given, encourage people to think about how understandable they were
- Which medium will you use to convey the message?
- What effect has it had? How will you gather feedback?

A.3 EQUIPMENT LIST FOR AN EFFECTIVE STUDY/WORKSHOP

The majority of studies will require that presentations are made, and all will need some equipment to record discussions and decisions. This checklist covers the most common requirements: care should always be taken when using checklists to ensure that the specific needs of the study are met.

- Study handbook, invitation and study information
- Paper, pens, whiteboards (interactive can be very useful), flipcharts, transparencies, highlighters
- Sticky notes, putty adhesive, drawing pins, sticky tape (all the aforementioned relate to what is available at the location)
- Consider the layout of the room when conducting presentations and workshops – if possible, visit the venue before compiling the handbook, as it may be that you will prefer to organize the study differently as a result
- Breakout spaces
- Data projector, connection leads
- Laptop and power lead, mouse, printer/fax if available
- Software, storage media
- General and study-specific presentation files
- Feedback from pre-study consultations and analysis
- Enlargements of function analysis (if available) or other material requiring close examination
- Attendance forms and evaluation forms

- Proposal development forms
- Sample report
- Refreshments.

A.4 INVITATION TO JOIN THE STUDY TEAM

Certain information is essential to ensure that participants are well prepared from the start:

- Name of the study
- Purpose of the study
- Scope of the study
- Outline of the process to be followed
- Location and timing of workshop (if one is planned to start the study)
- Agenda
- Specific instructions for preparation by participants
- Listing of what information should be contained in the handbook (see section A.9), which participants will need to be familiar with.

A.4.1 Pro forma invitation

Dear [name] [can be an individual or a group]

[State why the study is being held.] You have been selected as [nature of anticipated contribution].

I would therefore like to invite you to contribute to [name of study], with its first session [amend as necessary] on [date] at [location]. This workshop will be facilitated by [study leader]. It starts at [time] and finishes by [time] or by agreement with the team, depending on progress. [There may be more than one day spent at a time: if this is necessary, ensure that it is clearly stated.]

Please be on time: in this workshop each session builds upon earlier activities, so we simply cannot accept any late arrivals or premature departures. A detailed agenda is attached.

This study is an investment for [name of organization] and you must come prepared to gain maximum benefit from it. You should come with a completely open mind, ready to generate ideas and learn from those of others. Please locate and familiarize yourself with the following material:

- [Item]
- [Item]
- [Item].

I have no doubt that you will find this exercise highly beneficial and I look forward to seeing your contributions.

Regards,
[Sponsor]

A.5 OPTION EVALUATION MATRIX

Often it is necessary to choose between a few options to assess which provides best value for money. Table A.1 provides a format for doing this.

A.6 PLAN THE STUDY

There are a number of MoV studies commonly applicable to a given project, from need verification to project review. Each of these differs somewhat in its requirements, but a generic plan of activities for a single study will generally include the following:

- ■ Conduct briefing meeting
- ■ Compile study handbook
- ■ Invite contributors and contributions to the study
- ■ Hold workshops/consultations as necessary

Table A.1 An example of an option evaluation matrix

			Evaluation criteria (i.e. value drivers)									
			Criterion 1	Criterion 2	Criterion 3	Criterion 4	Criterion 5	Criterion 6	Criterion 7	Criterion 8		
No.	Option (and cost)	Criterion weight	A%	B%	C%	D%	E%	F%	G%	H%	Value score	Measure of value for money
1	Option A (cost)	Benefit ranking										
		Benefit ranking × criterion weight									Total for this option	= value score/ cost
2	Option B (cost)	Benefit ranking										
		Benefit ranking × criterion weight									Total for this option	= value score/ cost
3	Option C (cost)	Benefit ranking										
		Benefit ranking × criterion weight									Total for this option	= value score/ cost
4	Option D (cost)	Benefit ranking										
		Benefit ranking × criterion weight									Total for this option	= value score/ cost

Table continues

Table A.1 *continued*

			Evaluation criteria (i.e. value drivers)									
			Criterion 1	Criterion 2	Criterion 3	Criterion 4	Criterion 5	Criterion 6	Criterion 7	Criterion 8		
5	Option E (cost)	Benefit ranking										
		Benefit ranking × criterion weight									Total for this option	= value score/ cost
6	Option F (cost)	Benefit ranking										
		Benefit ranking × criterion weight									Total for this option	= value score/ cost
		Benefit ranking: 1 = poor; 2 = fair; 3 = good; 4 = excellent										

- Construct value profile or FAST diagram and value profile
- Select options (if this is a study objective)
- Identify areas with most potential to add value
- Generate ideas for value improvement
- Evaluate ideas and select a number for full proposal development
- Generate study report
- Monitor implementation of ideas.

A.7 RECORDING IDEA SELECTION

A method is needed to capture all ideas and evaluate them, so that a proportion can be selected for further development. The most important features to capture for any idea are the ways in which it offers improvement and to what extent. As there should be a good many ideas, the most convenient layout would include the following:

- Name of the study from which the idea comes
- Criteria for evaluation
- Method by which ideas are ranked
- A unique identifier for each idea (if possible, ensure that this incorporates an identifier for the study also – see cross-references below)
- Outline of the idea
- Ranking resulting from the evaluation process

- Estimated impacts (cost savings, extra value, others according to need)
- Cross-references to similar ideas. (NB: as time passes and more documentation is available in this format, it will be possible to cross-reference ideas from other studies. However, this is unlikely to be possible in the early stages.)

A.8 REPORTING STUDY OUTPUTS

The outcomes of an MoV study must always be recorded and fed back to its sponsors. This allows ideas to be progressed, implemented and learned from. Below is an outline for a generic MoV report, with all content that should be considered against its audience, i.e. not all parts will necessarily apply to all versions of the report.

- Project (if relevant) and/or study title
- Introduction, which needs to include:
  - Description of how the study fits into the context of the overall programme
  - Explanation of why the study or project is needed
  - Explanation of the purpose of the study
- List of those involved in the study, both internal and external to the organization
- Methodology followed, e.g. meetings, consultations

- Study process
- Information used by the study
- Information generated by the study, including analysis of consultations, presentations made and documents shared
- Summary of outcomes
- Details of value-improving proposals in progress, their owners and dates for delivery of a business case (where available).

A.9   SCOPING THE STUDY

The study scope documents the name and purpose of the study and lists the study sponsor and stakeholders. It also lists assumptions, constraints and givens. The primary source of information on these points is the briefing meeting.

- Assumptions: statements that are believed to be true. These can always be challenged by the team, but many will simply be statements of work that can be done elsewhere.
- Constraints: restrictions placed on the study, e.g. the outcome must conform to specific parameters. (See also 'theory of constraints' in Appendix B for a slightly different interpretation.)
- Givens: aspects of a study that are not open to challenge.
- Scope: area remaining to explore opportunities for challenge and improvement.

A suggested template for the study scope follows:

- [Study name]
- [Study objective]
- [Drivers for change] [Describe in business terms and in some detail.]
- [Key stakeholders] [List study sponsor and steering group.]
- [Other stakeholders] [Include their role in the study.]
- [Boundaries to the study] [State givens, assumptions and constraints with clear separation. If there are any dependencies on other studies/projects, state them here.]
- [Desired targets] [Again, described in business terms, preferably using the same measures as the drivers for change.]
- [Critical success factors].

A.10   STUDY OR WORKSHOP HANDBOOK

In order to function effectively, the study team will need certain guidelines and information. This is normally attached to the invitation and should be proportionate to the scale of the study. The study leader will use some of this information to decide how best to conduct the study. Most common items will include:

- The project brief, or terms of reference, incorporating the scope
- Study objectives and requirements
- Background to the development of these requirements
- Current performance information and any underlying issues
- Other information describing the current situation (this can include diagrams, organization charts, models, process flow charts etc.)
- Feasibility studies and option studies
- Revenue and cost information (capital, operating and whole-life costs)
- Feedback from existing project, if relevant, or feedback from similar studies
- Planning and other statutory approvals, if these are relevant
- List of study team members and communication plan, both within the study and to feed back to the rest of the organization
- Any other information identified in briefing meetings.

A.11   VALUE-IMPROVING PROPOSAL FORMS

Some sort of standard form is necessary for summarizing and presenting the outputs from a value study in a way that allows them to be compared. This means that they can be prioritized against available funds. Below is a checklist of items for inclusion in the template:

- Unique reference number
- Summary of the study from which the proposal originates
- Date of form generation and name of owner
- Reference of the idea generating the proposal and description of the idea
- Outline of the existing situation that the proposal is intended to improve, with the functions carried out

- Description of the proposed improvement and how it impacts on the functions stated above
- Advantages of the proposal
- Drawbacks of the proposal
- Costs, preferably on a whole-life basis
- Impacts on time, performance and other qualities
- Recommended implementation method
- Other solutions considered with their relative advantages and drawbacks
- Effects on normal output measures for this area (e.g. delivery time, supply cost, whole-life cost)
- Date presented for discussion
- Outline record of the discussion, with decision and supporting rationale.

Additional supporting information for clarity should be attached to the form.

A.12 VALUE IMPROVEMENT TRACKING REPORT

A suggested form for monitoring progress in implementing the agreed changes following a study is given in Table A.2.

It saves a great deal of time if this is run in a spreadsheet, with dropdown lists of the value drivers and owners etc. Also, it will be necessary to score how easy it is to implement, the likely capital investment (later, this will be the amount actually used) and the operating cost (whether or not this is a measure).

A high, medium, low scale is normal for implementation needs, with a calibration chart to indicate what this means. These three scores, combined with the authority to proceed, can be converted to a number that defines the colour in the status column. The virtue of a 'traffic light' chart is that it is simple to follow and can be published to management regularly with little difficulty. Once authority to proceed has been granted, a new unique identifier can be assigned, to distinguish the nature of that stage of implementation from later progress where the measures themselves are of more importance and can also be incorporated to the status measure.

Each of these changes, together with new proposals, can be built into a benefits realization plan, and monitoring can take place there, which avoids setting up a separate spreadsheet. The advantage of this (if benefits realization is a normal process for the organization) is that there will be somebody responsible for reviewing progress at regular intervals and the senior MoV practitioner can simply get information from them. Also, there is merit in all changes being tracked together.

The drawback is that these intervals are not under the senior MoV practitioner's control and might not correspond to the reporting schedule agreed with stakeholders, so duplication of effort may occur.

Table A.2 Example of a value improvement tracking report

Unique identifier	Idea synopsis	Value driver	Owners responsible for making the changes	Measure(s)	Implementation needs			Authority to proceed	Status
					Ease of doing	Capital investment	Operating cost		

Appendix B: Toolbox

Appendix B: Toolbox

This appendix offers a guide to the many tools and techniques that may be used with MoV. Those that are exclusive to MoV, such as function analysis, are explained in Chapter 4 rather than here, together with those that are very commonly used in MoV interventions.

The contents have been structured in alphabetical order and may be useful on several occasions within a study. This list is not exhaustive and the seasoned MoV practitioner may wish to include other techniques, particularly if these are sector specific.

Further information on most of these techniques and other references made elsewhere in this guide may be found at http://www.best-management-practice.com

Tool/technique	Outline of technique(s)	Benefits, implementation points and signposts
Business process re-engineering	Business process re-engineering takes a 'clean-slate' approach to processes and redesigns them for greater effectiveness. Its strength and its weakness both lie in its single focus on process: interfaces with other factors need to be explored for this technique to allow costs to be reduced, or quality, service and speed to be increased without reducing the organization's overall value.	www.training-management.info/BPR.htm offers an outline of how to carry out BPR.
Conjoint analysis	Offers customers choices of different combinations of features or service levels to compile preferences.	Useful in situations demanding a prediction of respondent choices, it is usually conducted on the basis of a questionnaire.
Cost estimation	Methods of estimating capital and whole-life costs.	Useful information is contained at www.dfpni.gov.uk/eag_principles_of_cost_measurement and also www.ogc.gov.uk/implementing_plans_introduction_life_cycle_costing_.asp
De Bono P/M/I	The 'P/M/I' in this technique stands for 'Plus/Minus/Interesting'. Put each of these headings at the top of a column, then for each idea, put all the positive effects its implementation will have (the pluses), in the next the negatives (the minuses) and any other effects whose impact is uncertain in the third column.	A technique to ensure that the idea being proposed is actually likely to lead to improvement. See www.mindtools.com for further information.
Delphi	A method of getting groups of individuals to arrive at consensus without face-to-face discussion. A panel of contributors is asked for their opinions in a series of questionnaires by the study leader, but none of them knows the opinions of the others.	Avoids groupthink (where dissent is suppressed by peer pressure), although this method can suffer from poor questioning or analysis. Can also be used to gain consensus from a set of disparate data. See www.unido.org/fileadmin/import/16959_DelphiMethod.pdf

Table continues

Tool/technique	Outline of technique(s)	Benefits, implementation points and signposts
Dots	A simple method to get the team to gauge relative importance is for the study leader to specify the number of favourite ideas that each team member can select (ideally, this will be about 20–30% of the total) and give them sticky dots to put against each of these ideas. The number of dots against each idea selected is totalled, with the one with the most dots being ranked most important and so on.	Whilst hardly scientific, this can be a very effective method to assign relative importance. It can be used to select ideas for further development.
Earned value analysis or management	Method of assessing whether a project is on track for completion within agreed time and cost targets. Despite its name, it is not a specific MoV technique, but a project control method.	www.apmg-international.com/home/Qualifications/EVMQuals.asp A detailed explanation is given at www.projectsmart.co.uk/earned-value-management-explained.html
Elementary skills gap analysis	Comparing the skills that are needed for a task with those available in the project or study team with a view to filling any gaps by training or inviting additional members. This can be detailed and costly on an organizational level. However, for the purposes of an MoV study or programme thereof, it should be sufficient for the study leader to consider, with the steering group, what skills are required. Then, as each individual team member is recommended, ask how their skills fit with this. Alternatively, ask the team member. Eventually, a list of weaknesses that need to be addressed will be formed.	It is worth noting that training only addresses lack of knowledge. Mentoring and coaching may be preferable for improving competence and attitude. Other ideas can be found in http://skill-assessment.suite101.com/article.cfm/skill_gap_analysis There is also extra information at www.ehow.co.uk/about_5451842_skill-gap-analysis.html
Excursions and metaphors	Taking delegates offsite (excursion) to an area where creativity flourishes. The return journey often generates a great many ideas.	Can be very effective, especially as a precursor to brainstorming or idea generation tools.
Facilitation	This is specialist mix of knowledge and intuition. It is the subject of much MoV training.	www.executivebrief.com/blogs/10-tips-to-boost-your-facilitation-skills has some useful tips. For those who feel in need of detailed information, try www.iaf-world.org/i4a/pages/index.cfm?pageid=3280 (for members only).
Five Ws and an H	Extends the depth of questioning when exploring a problem. Simply asks a series of questions for each process, starting with: • Who? • Why? • What? • When? • Where? • How?	Deceptively simple, this technique forces a more organized challenge to existing processes and product designs and can generate much innovation. It also has the great virtue of being readily understood. www.scribd.com/doc/3666200/5W1H-Who-What-Where-When-Why-How has other comments about this technique, which are useful for further exploration.

Tool/technique	Outline of technique(s)	Benefits, implementation points and signposts
Function Analysis System Technique (FAST)	A diagrammatic representation of functions and their hierarchy, FAST works by asking how the functions relate to each other. There are three main forms: • Traditional: designed to describe what the component parts of the study subject must do. It can be applied at any level. • Technical: similar to traditional FAST, aimed mainly at products and widely used in manufacturing. It is generally used at subsystem or component levels. • Customer: focuses on customer requirements. Functions describe what the customer expects to get, rather than exactly what it does.	See www-users.aston.ac.uk/~gus/notes/lect8.pdf
Function priority matrix	Method of keeping the simplicity of conventional function analysis, whilst minimizing the time it takes, by sorting functions according to whether they are strategic or tactical and how essential they are to the organization.	The original article on this topic can be found at www.value-solutions.co.uk/Function%20Priority%20 Matrix%20v2.pdf
HM Treasury's *Green Book*	MoV provides the means to maximize benefits and minimize waste and resources needed to deliver to expectations. MoV utilizes many of the methods described in the *Green Book* and thus provides consistency of approach.	See www.hm-treasury.gov.uk/data_greenbook_ guidance.htm
Information-gathering methods	There will always be large volumes of data available to a study, but time will be at a premium. Therefore, you need to understand the purpose of the study before you start, and this is normally set by the briefing meeting. It is useful to correlate some information from this important source (as with others) against other sources to ensure a full picture for the study team. When consulting, the best way is generally to talk to people one–to-one, or in groups. Questionnaires are also extremely useful if large numbers of people are involved.	A checklist of questions for use at the strategic briefing meeting is held in Appendix A. Useful (if rather thorough) lists of considerations can be found at www.lboro.ac.uk/service/ltd/campus/ infouser.pdf – this is aimed predominantly at students, but the principles contained are equally applicable to other settings. *See also* www.eastdevon.gov.uk/plg-pp-consultation.pdf for a neat paper that describes methods of consultation with the general public, if this is relevant to your study. www.statpac.com/surveys gives a good deal of information about compiling questionnaires and surveys.
Issues generation and analysis	Team members write down their issues on sticky notes and display them on a wall grouped under appropriate headings, e.g. Assumptions, Constraints, or Opportunities. Team members then vote for their top 10 and can explore ways to address these issues.	This has the virtue of narrowing focus to a relatively small area, but the consequence is potentially to overlook a major opportunity elsewhere.

Table continues

Tool/technique	Outline of technique(s)	Benefits, implementation points and signposts
Kano quality model	An improvement philosophy showing continuous evolution of performance and quality, whereby yesterday's innovations become today's performance differentiators and tomorrow's essential attributes. May be used in conjunction with the MoV knowledge database.	An article demonstrating application of Kano can be found at www.isixsigma.com/index. php?option=com_k2&view=item&id=1116:&Item id=206
Knowledge capture and dissemination	Data is a collection of words or numbers. Information is data placed in context. Knowledge is using information and applying it to your organization. Knowledge capture involves recording information (following an MoV study or programme of studies) that can inform future learning and performance improvement. Methods of dissemination will vary according to the organization.	This is an enormous topic. A good grounding can be found at http://eprints.aktors.org/44/01/valuation-methods.pdf (there are also many books). A more advanced understanding can be had from *Information Technology for Knowledge Management* by Uwe M Borghoff and Remo Pareschi (Springer, 1998) (this publication assumes familiarity with the basics). For application of Nonaka's Socialization, Externalization, Combination and Internalization (SECI Model (separating explicit and tacit knowledge by tacit and explicit methods of acquiring it) to programme management, go to www2.warwick.ac. uk/fac/soc/wbs/conf/olkc/archive/oklc4/papers/ oklc2003_wickes.pdf Guidance on assessing trends is given at http:// trendwatching.com/tips, although its focus is on external consumer data and some tailoring is required. Additional information on PEST (political, economic, social and technological) analysis (and related ideas) is given at www.jiscinfonet.ac.uk/tools/ scenario-planning/trend-analysis.
Lean principles and Lean Sigma	Lean methodologies have become very popular, owing to the inherent attractiveness of their focus on the customer. However, they do require total commitment from an organization, as they cannot be implemented effectively at a local level owing to the need to interface with other areas. This makes them high risk in comparison with MoV, although they deliver high reward if they pay off.	www.valuestreamguru.com/?p=108 is interesting.
Managing difficult people	This is a large topic to cover here, so a list of texts is offered. Key points to remember are: • Behaviours are sometimes driven by a desire to get the job done. This isn't necessarily bad. • Understand the effects of this behaviour, good and bad, and the personalities that manifest as a result. • Recognize when what you do triggers adverse behaviour in another.	A concise publication is *Dealing with Difficult People* by Dr Rick Brinkman and Dr Rick Kirschner (McGraw-Hill, 2006). http://business.timesonline.co.uk/tol/business/ management/article6011177.ece is an interesting article on this subject. The Chartered Institute of Personnel and Development has *Handling Difficult People and Difficult Situations* by Greg Whitear and Geoff Ribbens, available at www.cipd.co.uk/Bookstore/_ catalogue/Training/9781843981756.htm

Tool/technique	Outline of technique(s)	Benefits, implementation points and signposts
Net present value	The final output of a discounted cash flow analysis.	Details of calculation can be found from many sources, including the *Green Book*.
Pareto	Method of selecting the areas of a subject with most potential for value enhancement. Often called the 80/20 rule, where 80% of the impact is made by the top 20% of ideas.	Maximizes return on time where it is scarce. It has the drawback of sometimes operating on incomplete information, so sometimes missing significant opportunities.
Peer review	Process of seeking objective inputs or comments from similarly qualified individuals who are impartial to the subject or project under study.	This can be an excellent method of gaining feedback on strengths and weaknesses for the subject under study, allowing for constructive challenge and recommended solutions to be made.
Presentation techniques	Hints and tips for preparing and giving presentations (signposts).	www.presentationmagazine.com/presentationtips. htm contains a massive amount of information.
Report writing	An outline for an MoV study report has been given in Appendix A.	www.samples-help.org.uk/report-writing/index.htm provides a basic list of things to remember (albeit surrounded by adverts), based on use of MSWord.
Risk management	The systematic application of principles, approaches and processes to the tasks of identifying and assessing risks and then planning and implementing risk responses.	See *Management of Risk* (M_o_R), published by TSO/OGC or www.hm-treasury.gov.uk/orange_book.htm or ISO 31000 www.iso.org/iso/catalogue_detail. htm?csnumber=43170
SCAMPER	This is a mnemonic to aid idea generation: Substitute Combine Amend Modify Put to other use Expand Reverse/reduce	This can help with crossing the bridge from a creative thought to a practicable idea, or to expand the concept behind an idea. It also encourages different ways of expressing the same idea, which can provoke new ones. Further information is available at www.mindtools.com/pages/article/ newCT_02.htm
Scenario building	Analysing the relative effectiveness of value enhancement of various combinations of proposals according to a specified view of future conditions.	A description of scenario-planning and associated techniques can be found at www.jiscinfonet.ac.uk/ tools/scenario-planning/scenario-planning.pdf
SMART – Simple Multi-Attribute Rating Technique	A technique for use during the briefing and outline design stages of building developments.	A SMART Methodology for Value Management, Chartered Institute of Building, Occasional Paper No 53, 1992
Soft systems methodology (SSM)	Compares the current situation with the ideal situation to generate acceptable actions for change. It has gained a large following in information systems and is very useful for managing conflicting stakeholder objectives, although its use of jargon is a barrier.	*Soft Systems Methodology in Action* by Peter Checkland (John Wiley & Sons, 1999)

Table continues

Tool/technique	Outline of technique(s)	Benefits, implementation points and signposts
Stakeholder analysis	Identification of those people or organizations with a vested interest in a project, product, service or process and their attitudes towards it. This analysis also indicates their levels of interest and the influence they may exert.	Explains how best to engage with these people or organizations. It can assist in focusing attention on satisfying key stakeholder interests. Principles are discussed in this guide. The definitive process is given by *Managing Successful Programmes* (MSP) and reference to this publication is recommended.
Stakeholder identification	Whilst in many cases the stakeholders are clearly visible, this is not always the case. Some guidance is offered in Chapter 4.	MSP is the leading guide on this subject, and www.guild.demon.co.uk/ProjectSociology.pdf also has some very interesting material on this topic.
Strategic choice approach	Works through four stages (shaping, designing, comparing and choosing), focusing on the uncertainties inherent in the decision under review. As it is a framework, it works well with MoV. It uses three stages (or modes): shaping a problem, designing alternative responses and comparing these responses to select the best.	*Planning Under Pressure* (Urban and Regional Planning series) by John Friend and Alan Hickling (Elsevier Butterworth Heinemann, 2005).
Strategic options development and analysis (SODA)	A cognitive and causal mapping tool to aid understanding of strategic options and their consequences; it is especially helpful for messy, complex problems.	An explanation of operational research and SODA's role in it can be found at http://people.brunel.ac.uk/~mastjjb/jeb/or/softor.html
Sustainability and triple bottom line	A term coined by John Elkington, the triple bottom line approach ensures that the economic, environmental and social impacts of proposals are taken into account. Methods of doing this will inevitably vary, as do accounting policies themselves. The most important feature of whatever methods are selected is that, like the comment under value metrics, they must be seen to be transparent and objective.	*The Durable Corporation: strategies for sustainable development* by G Aras and D Crowther (Gower, 2009). www.johnelkington.com/TBL-elkington-chapter.pdf contains the original article. www.censa.org.uk/docs/Wiedmann_Lenzen_2006_SDRC_paper.pdf gives some insights into reporting methods.
SWOT analysis	SWOT stands for strengths, weaknesses, opportunities and threats. It is an aid to developing MoV plans.	A commonplace tool to focus activities on areas with growth potential and minimize any shortcomings in an organization.
Systems thinking	Most methodologies involve analysing a problem into its constituent parts and their properties to extend understanding. Systems thinking focuses on the relationships between these constituents formed by their combination. It has been used very effectively and works well with MoV.	www.reallylearning.com/Free_Resources/Systems_Thinking/systems_thinking.html contains a useful introduction to this subject.
Target costing	Sets target costs based on what the market will pay for something, rather than how much it costs to produce it.	www.cimaglobal.com/Documents/ImportedDocuments/ReformingtheNHSfromwithin.pdf treats this subject comprehensively.

Tool/technique	Outline of technique(s)	Benefits, implementation points and signposts
T charts	A simple technique which places positive outcomes on one side of a sheet and negative on the other. A statement of the idea forms the top of the T.	
Team-building	Much material is available for further study, although it can be difficult to separate the information from the plethora of training courses and team-building games that are publicized. Reference to the material cited will signpost many other resources.	*Team Building: Proven Strategies for Improving Team Performance* by E Schein and W Dyer (Wiley, 2007). http://www.tms.com.au/tms12-1i.html presents a research article bringing together work from other professionals. http://hbr.org/product/managing-teams-for-high-performance/an/2304-PDF-ENG offers a series of articles on this subject.
Theory of constraints	The theory of constraints contends that any manageable system is limited in achieving more of its goal by a very small number of constraints, and that there is always at least one constraint.	A considerable amount of information can be found at www.answers.com/topic/theory-of-constraints
Tracking benefits realization	Benefits arising from MoV proposals may need to be monitored during or after project completion, or as a change to business as usual. Methods need to be able to span a considerable period of time (often years) in order that individual benefits can be tracked, quantified and promulgated within an organization. A plan needs to be constructed to show what is expected, where and when, with a named person responsible for making it happen. Whatever method is used must be sufficiently objective to stand up to independent review.	Sections 7.8, 7.9 and 7.10 in *Managing Successful Programmes* are very relevant. Also *Benefit Realisation Management* by Gerald Bradley (Gower, 2010) is helpful. Guidance regarding potential pitfalls is held at www.cimaglobal.com/Thought-leadership/Newsletters/Insight-e-magazine/Insight-2010/Insight-March-2010/Realising-benefits-of-business-change--challenge-1
Value metrics	Methods of measuring monetary and non-monetary value enhancements. When setting metrics, it is preferable that they should be as objective as possible and essential that existing reporting systems are capable of producing them regularly.	A breakdown of performance management, which is closely allied, is available at www.businessballs.com/dtiresources/performance_measurement_management.pdf
Warm-up exercises/ ice breakers	Ways to relax participants and encourage collaboration and a sense of 'team'.	Information can be found at www.mindtools.com/pages/article/newLDR_76.htm
Workshop/study toolkit	See Appendix A for a checklist to support studies and/or their workshops.	

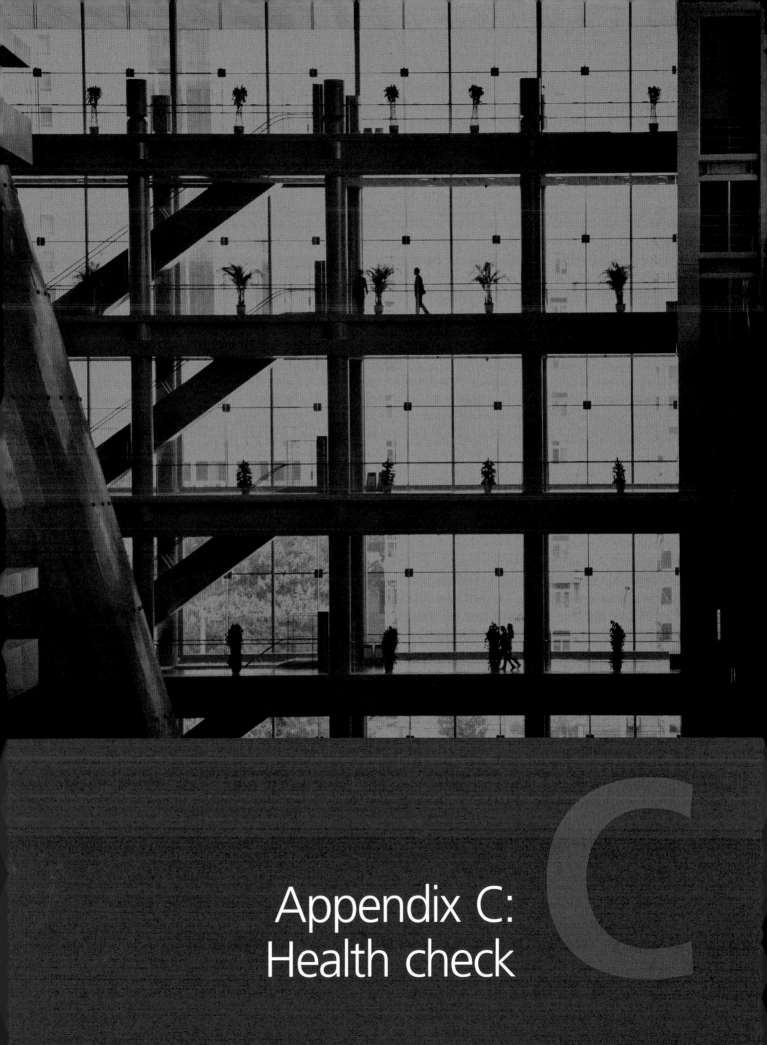

Appendix C:
Health check

Appendix C: Health check

C.1 PURPOSE

Chapter 7 describes the processes involved in introducing and embedding MoV into an organization. To maintain and improve the practice and culture of MoV it is necessary to undertake regular maintenance of the processes that have been put in place so that they are continually refreshed.

The health check is designed to review the status of MoV across the organization, assess its effectiveness and diagnose where it might be improved. It should be refined as organizations become more experienced in the use of MoV.

Regular health checks may also be used to develop plans for increasing organizational or individual maturity which is discussed in Appendix D.

Health checks may be applied at organizational, programme, project or operational levels.

The frequency of undertaking health checks should be described in the MoV implementation plan.

A health check may be useful:

- As a regular review of the embedding of MoV to protect the original investment and realize the full potential benefits from that investment
- As an integral part of business planning activity
- When preparing annual operating plans
- When considering a significant investment or embarking on a major project or programme
- In response to major changes that may be required, for example by changes in legislation
- As part of the preparation for OGC Gateway Reviews
- As part of the process of improving MoV maturity.

C.2 PROCESS

The process for undertaking health checks at any level should form part of the MoV plan but, in general, should include the following steps.

C.2.1 Preparation

The health check should be initiated by the senior MoV practitioner with the support of the support office, if available or, since it is effectively a quality check, those charged with quality assurance. The senior MoV practitioner should appoint a health check team leader if not leading the review personally.

The first task is to set the terms of reference, the objectives, the scope and the timing of the exercise

Next, select a suitable review team or individual (hereafter referred to as the team to avoid repetition) and define the roles and responsibilities of those involved.

The review team leader will then brief the team, including refining the health check process to fit the specific circumstances, explaining the structure, the reasons for it and the outputs that are sought.

The team will develop questions that are specific to the aspect of MoV under check and the purpose of the health check, using the questions listed under the framework (see section C.3) as a basis. Questions should be open wherever possible to force a response to be based on supporting evidence.

The review team leader should identify who should interview whom, develop a schedule of interviews, identify any other sources of information and how best to capture them.

The review team or individual will then gather information on the aspect of MoV that is being checked (this could, for example, be the status of its embedding over the organization or how it is set up for a major project or programme).

The review team leader should plan the format of the report and its audience. Once the review is complete, the report should be compiled and submitted to the appropriate people.

C.2.2 Data collection

The team should review the written documentation such as the project MoV plan, seeking additional information if necessary, make notes on the responses and discussion topics arising from the interviews and seek out additional information as required to fill any gaps that become apparent.

C.2.3 Data analysis

The team should then identify strengths, weaknesses, opportunities and threats and analyse responses using a SWOT analysis and identify trends and patterns.

If the health check is being used to improve maturity, the team should assess steps needed to achieve this (see Appendix D).

The review team leader should then develop findings and recommendations, and draft an implementation plan.

C.2.4 Report and review

The review team leader will then compile a report outlining the processes followed, the findings and recommendations and present these, together with the draft implementation plan to the senior MoV practitioner or the sponsor.

Following the review with the senior MoV practitioner or sponsor, the review team leader will finalize and submit the report.

C.2.5 Implementation

Implementation of the recommendations in the report will be undertaken by suitable people in the organization, who should be identified in the implementation plan. The senior MoV practitioner should brief those who are responsible for following through on the recommendations so that they understand and can act on the implementation plan.

The senior MoV practitioner will also define the mechanism for monitoring implementation progress and changing the plans as necessary to maximize the benefits arising from the investment in the health check.

C.3 FRAMEWORK

This framework provides a checklist of questions upon which to build, structured around the seven principles of MoV. Figure C.1 indicates how performance against each principle may be assessed in line with the organizational maturity, discussed in Appendix D

The health check is conducted by assessing responses to a number of questions that relate to each MoV principle, built upon the examples set out below, and should be open to discussion if possible.

Affirmative responses confirm that an aspect of each of the principles has been applied. Negative or equivocal responses indicate that the aspect is not fully applied, if at all. Sometimes a question may lead to a discussion on a related topic. Such discussion can be extremely useful in diagnosing areas for improvement and should be recorded.

It is important that the questions are answered realistically; reflecting actual circumstances, rather than being skewed to what people may believe is the 'right answer'. A number of peers from different parts of the organization should be involved in the review to provide an objective 'peer review' of the status to avoid overly optimistic and misleading interpretations of the status of MoV practice.

Questions under each principle should be selected and adapted to suit the specific requirements of the health check. This should be done by the leader of the health check rather than the heath check team members. Where applicable, the questions should probe expertise, experience and capability at business, programme, project and operational levels, whether or not this is explicit in the lists below.

Some of these questions may need to be amended if the organization is running agile projects.

C.3.1 Align with organizational objectives

Consideration: how is MoV applied to strategic, programme, project and operational issues in the context of the organization's objectives?

Possible questions to pose:

- How do the MoV policy and plan reflect the organization's objectives and priorities?
- Are these represented by an organizational value profile?
- Do the MoV policy and plan make it clear which activities should be routinely subjected to MoV and when?
- Where have the organization's value priorities been defined and are they current?
- Has the management team fully bought into the policy and plan?
- How are senior management kept informed of the effectiveness of the MoV activities?
- Have the programme/project objectives been defined in a simple SMART manner such that all involved in its delivery have access to it and can understand it?

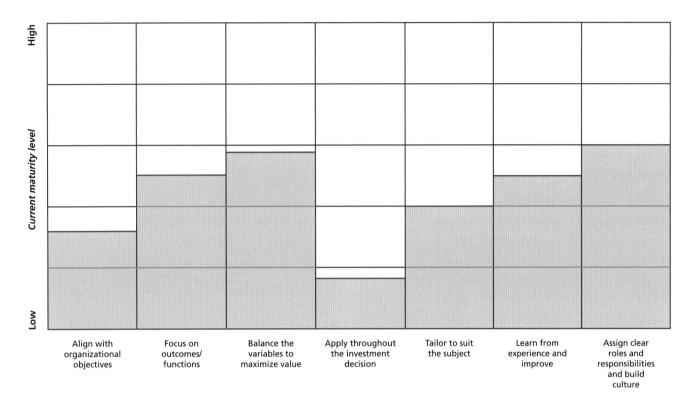

Figure C.1 MoV maturity histogram

- How do the programme or project objectives relate to the organization's business objectives?
- How has it been demonstrated that the programme/project is the best way in which to deliver the expected benefits?
- What is the method that the organization adopts to inform the MoV team of changes in programme or project objectives and the resultant changes in the brief?
- How are project objectives within a programme coordinated to contribute to the programme objectives?
- Are decisions at all levels based on value?

C.3.2 Focus on function and required outcomes

Consideration: are MoV activities firmly based on identifying the functional requirements of programme and project objectives?

Possible questions to pose:

- Are programme and project objectives expressed in a SMART format stating the required outcomes rather than outputs?
- Does the organization understand the concept of value drivers (functions that are, in aggregate, necessary and sufficient to deliver the programme or project objectives in full)?
- Are members of the organization familiar with the concepts of function as applied in MoV?
- Do people recognize that not all benefits have a monetary value, and how do they take account of these?
- What types of function diagram are used to express business, programme, project or operational values?
- How does the organization demonstrate that it strives to maximize value for money?
- How are different stakeholders' value priorities captured and shared?
- Are function diagrams used to encourage innovation and development of value-improving proposals?
- Has the organization developed generic value drivers that may be refined to suit individual circumstances for the projects it frequently carries out?
- When making decisions based on value, are all value and cost drivers assessed?
- How are design standards and quality aspirations expressed?

C.3.3 Balance the variables to maximize value

Consideration: maximizing overall value requires that three sets of variables are balanced to achieve the optimum outcome. The sets of variables are: benefits gained against resources used, reconciliation of benefits according to different stakeholders' priorities and achieving the optimum balance between the use of money, materials and time.

Possible questions to pose:

- Is the concept of the value ratio well understood throughout the organization?
- What is the organization's approach to identifying and managing stakeholders?
- Have the senior management visibly given their support to embedding and improving MoV?
- Have the main stakeholders who may have an impact on the project, both internally and externally, been identified?
- Have the stakeholders, including the end users, been consulted in arriving at the project objectives?
- Has their attitude, interest and influence on the project been analysed and an engagement plan been developed?
- How are differing stakeholder expectations managed?
- How do people deal with widely differing stakeholder expectations at project, programme and business levels?
- How is the optimum balance between differing stakeholder expectations, including environmental and community policies, expressed?
- Are the organization's priorities across time, cost and quality clearly understood?
- What methods are used to balance the use of time, money, energy and materials?
- Is the organization's sustainability policy clearly understood?
- What methods are used to optimize the balance between the delivery of benefits and the use of resources?
- Are decisions based on clear statements of value for the organization and their maximization?
- Do the teams use scenarios to maximize value?
- How are resources balanced to maximize value on a project?

- Are project reviews conducted at key milestones and at the end of the project to assess the effectiveness of incorporating the value-improving proposals and the resulting improvements in value?
- How are improvements in value, taking account of monetary and non-monetary benefits, measured and monitored?

C.3.4 Apply throughout the programme or project

Consideration: are MoV activities planned and delivered at all project stages?

Possible questions to pose:

- Are the different management stages clearly identified from the outset?
- Are the different technical stages clearly identified from the outset?
- Are the MoV activities for each management or technical stage identified from the outset?
- Are the MoV activities and necessary, appropriate, resources clearly identified on the master schedule?
- Are the MoV team members competent and experienced in conducting MoV studies at all the relevant milestones and stages, taking into account the different focus for these activities?
- Are appropriate MoV activities planned for OGC Gateway Reviews and other key programme or project milestones?
- Is MoV used regularly as part of project reviews, including post-project reviews, to assess performance and ascertain whether expected benefits were delivered?
- Is MoV used to improve operational performance after a project has been commissioned or to improve operational performance for 'business as usual'?
- Are the value-improving proposals and the status of their incorporation in the project included in the regular project reports and reviewed at project meetings?

C.3.5 Tailor to suit the programme or project

Consideration: the extent and depth of MoV involvement should be adjusted to suit the circumstances to achieve maximum value whilst avoiding unnecessary process-driven activities. It is vital to avoid 'tick-box' activities.

Possible questions to pose:

- What methods are employed to assess the level of effort and resources to be deployed in MoV activities at each stage throughout a project?
- Are MoV practitioners familiar with a broad range of MoV involvement to suit the circumstances?
- MoV includes a range of techniques. How do practitioners select what is appropriate for the circumstances?
- In a programme comprising multiple projects, how is an appropriate balance of MoV activity assessed across each contributing project?
- How is MoV integrated with other project management activities?
- Does the MoV plan clearly set out the circumstances and levels of MoV that should be applied?

C.3.6 Learn from experience and improve

Consideration: are there strategies in place for continuous performance improvement and is their implementation achieving results?

Possible questions to pose:

- Is there a person responsible and accountable for improving MoV practice across the organization?
- What processes are in place to learn and share lessons learned between similar projects or projects within a programme?
- How do you gauge the level of MoV effort needed for individual projects?
- How do your MoV practitioners improve their competence from new to experienced practitioner?
- Is there a system in place for improving individual practitioners' personal competence?
- Is regular feedback received from practitioners to improve processes and techniques?
- Are MoV processes reviewed against a maturity model to determine the maturity level and the resulting benefits that may be expected?
- How often do you update your written processes to keep pace with advances in MoV practice?
- How do your MoV practitioners ensure that they are familiar with the latest developments in MoV?

- How do you adapt your MoV processes and techniques to improve performance and ensure that you are reflecting best management practice?
- How do you allow individual MoV practitioners to tailor their techniques to suit their characters whilst remaining consistent with MoV principles?
- Is the maturity of MoV practice improving?
- Is individual MoV competence monitored and reviewed?
- Is there a plan in place for progressing MoV maturity from one level to the next for the organization and individuals?
- Is the plan resourced and being actively managed?
- Is there a culture that encourages continual raising of the MoV bar by learning and disseminating known measures that improve value and by constantly seeking new ones?
- Is MoV practice included in the criteria for the relevant staff to advance their careers?
- What system do you have in place for recording lessons learned and enabling easy sharing of both factual and tacit knowledge to improve individual and organizational performance in MoV?
- How do you avoid MoV becoming a 'tick-box' activity?
- Are key value-improving proposals captured and disseminated within the organization to benefit other similar projects?

C.3.7 Assign clear roles and responsibilities and build culture

Consideration: in common with all management activities, it is vital that individuals' roles and responsibilities are clear. For MoV to be effective, it is essential that a culture exists that supports and encourages the maximization of value. Are roles clear and does the appropriate culture thrive?

Possible questions to pose:

- Is there a properly structured management approach to implementing MoV that includes key roles and responsibilities, a policy and plan for its implementation?
- Is there a dedicated sponsor for MoV with direct access to the executive board?
- Are the named individuals in the MoV plan truly accountable?

- Is there a centre of excellence that can provide appropriate support for the delivery of the tools and techniques?
- Have the management team bought fully into the MoV policy and plan?
- Are senior management in regular communication with the delivery of MoV?
- Are all staff aware of the roles they should play in the effective application of MoV?
- Are there clear guidelines and criteria in place for the selection of those who will be involved in the introduction, embedding and delivery of the MoV programme?
- Is there a programme in place to bring about necessary changes in attitude and behaviour to deliver the MoV programme?
- Is delivery of value for money reinforced by the examples set by line managers' behaviours and explicit MoV-related reward systems?
- Are clear MoV roles defined for all organizational objectives including all programme, project and operational activities?
- Are there clear guidelines in place on how to report proposals to improve value and learn lessons to continuously improve performance?
- Are roles and responsibilities for delivering MoV processes clearly articulated and defined?
- Are the required qualifications and capabilities of those responsible for MoV delivery and reporting clearly defined?

- Who is responsible for ensuring that the implementation of the value-improving proposals is monitored and the benefits realized?
- Are MoV delivery actions allocated to appropriate parties? Is the effectiveness of delivery monitored?
- Are the recommendations contained in this guide communicated to those involved in the setting up and delivery of the MoV programme?
- Can the organization apply MoV across all sectors of their activities?
- How has the organization demonstrated that it can apply MoV at business, programme, project and operational levels?
- Is there a culture embedded in the organization to challenge the status quo, to innovate and develop new ways to do things, and to overcome possible resistance?
- How are the organization's value priorities articulated and disseminated to all levels of management and staff?
- Is MoV integrated into key planning activities?
- How are management and staff encouraged, incentivized and committed to improve value for money?

Appendix D: Maturity
and competence

Appendix D: Maturity and competence

D.1 INTRODUCTION

Appendix C refers to the use of maturity modelling in assessing the health of MoV applications within an organization. The purpose of this Appendix is to introduce the concept of maturity models with particular reference to the OGC P3M3 model. Organizations should tailor and develop these models as they gain experience in the use of MoV.

P3M3 relates to the maturity of portfolio/programme/project processes as applied across an organization. It is also useful to assess the maturity of individual MoV study leaders if the organization has opted to use internal resource for this purpose. This section therefore also introduces a method of assessing individuals' MoV maturity.

Regular use of the organizational maturity model can provide the basis for setting long-term goals for MoV and coordinating it with other ways of measuring business performance. At the highest level of maturity, the business will be focused on optimizing its key processes based on quantitative measurement and aligned with business strategy and the external business environment.

The individual competence model is intended for assessing an individual's capabilities and the type of MoV study for which they are suited. A fully but recently qualified practitioner will lack the experience to undertake studies on particularly complex projects or programmes, particularly those where human or cultural factors may be significant. An initial period of acting as assistant study leader will improve competence to the point where the practitioner will be able to lead studies unaided. Further experience will render the practitioner able to lead more complex studies and to operate at programme and project levels.

D.2 PROCESS IMPROVEMENT

Embedding MoV in an organization, as discussed in Chapter 7, will require investment. The full benefits and the potential of that investment and the resulting competitive advantage will not be realized unless the organization strives to continually improve performance. Maturity models provide a widely recognized method of assessing progress in improving process delivery.

D.3 DEFINITION

The P3M3 maturity model is designed to provide a means of progressing towards realistic and achievable organizational goals. In the descriptions below, we have aligned P3M3 with how it might be applied to MoV.

Essentially, a maturity model is a structured group of attributes that together describe the characteristics of an effective process.

The MoV maturity model comprises five levels:

- **Level 1 – Awareness process** The organization recognizes that there are processes for maximizing value that could exist and should be followed but there is no consistency in approach, allocated roles and responsibilities or process across the organization.
- **Level 2 – Repeatable process** The organization has some developed standard methods to apply MoV, but those that exist are not consistently applied across the organization.
- **Level 3 – Defined process** There is a standard set of methods to apply MoV across the organization, which are consistently applied with clear process ownership.
- **Level 4 – Managed process** The organization captures the outputs from the MoV activities, monitors and measures them so that it can establish process efficiency quantitatively with a view to improving and optimizing performance.
- **Level 5 – Optimized process** The organization aligns its optimized delivery of MoV with its business needs, other key processes and the changing environment within which it operates and adjusts delivery accordingly.

It should be noted that not all organizations will be able to or need to achieve level 5 maturity in all MoV principles. The target levels should be set out in the MoV policy and plan, together with the reasons for selecting the target levels. Often level 3 maturity will be adequate to achieve value for money on most projects, and striving to achieve higher levels may, in itself, not represent the best use of management time and resources. The target should be related to the value added to the organization.

D.4 PURPOSE

As outlined above, the purpose of the MoV maturity model is to allow organizations to assess their MoV performance against objective criteria.

D.5 STRUCTURE

The MoV maturity model mimics the P3M3 structure outlined in Figure D.1.

Table D.1 shows the maturity levels described above and suitable attributes to explore to assess an organization's maturity.

Individual questions relating to each maturity step may be developed for each of the seven fundamental principles of MoV to explore the attributes outlined above:

- Align with organizational objectives
- Focus functions and required outcomes
- Balance the variables to maximize value
- Apply throughout the programme or project
- Tailor to suit the subject
- Learn from experience and improve
- Assign clear roles and responsibilities and build a supportive culture.

D.6 USE AND DEPLOYMENT

D.6.1 Progressing between maturity levels

Once MoV maturity has been assessed, it should be possible to identify what is needed to progress to the next level. This will require management time and effort, and the steps should be included in the MoV plan by the senior MoV practitioner. An example of the steps that may be needed in the plan to move from level 2 to level 3 is given below:

- Develop MoV processes that are tailored to suit the organization.
- Assess the organization's key objectives in managing value.

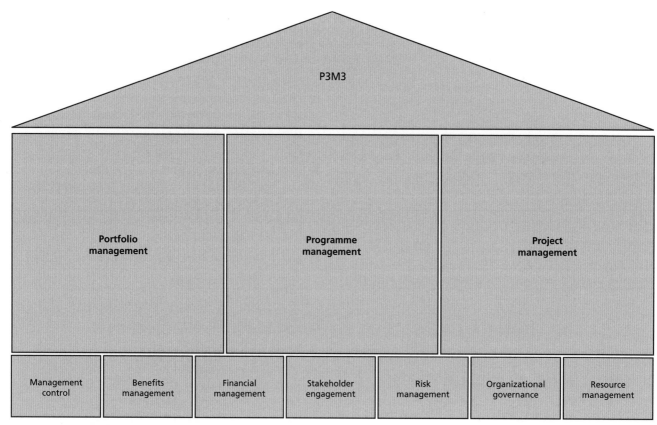

Figure D.1 P3M3 maturity structure

Table D.1 Outline MoV maturity model

MoV principle	Level 1	Level 2	Level 3	Level 4	Level 5
MoV overall	There is minimal evidence of MoV being used to any beneficial effect on projects. There may be evidence of efforts to reduce costs, but no formal process for retaining or enhancing benefits.	Formal MoV processes are recognized and used on projects, but there are inconsistent approaches, which result in different levels of commitment and effectiveness.	There are centrally defined processes for MoV that are used on all projects, people are cognizant of the organization's policy for the management of value, and MoV processes are used consistently.	MoV is working effectively, is embedded, and the resulting added value can be demonstrated. There is evidence of MoV being applied to strategic, programme, project and operational issues, and measured outputs are reported to senior management.	MoV is embedded in the organizational culture and underpins all decision-making within programmes and projects. There is evidence of continual improvement.
Possible attributes to look for	MoV is applied on an ad hoc basis by people who have no formal training. There is no uniform approach across the organization. Even where written processes do exist, they are not followed rigorously.	There are written procedures for most processes and training is available. Application of the processes varies across the organization. There are fewer than, say, five study leaders (depending upon the size of the organization and demand for MoV) with the experience and/or qualifications to deliver the services across a broad range of circumstances.	Written procedures and the delivery thereof are centrally managed. Records are kept of the outputs from MoV studies. There are more than, say, five (depending upon the size of the organization and demand for MoV) experienced and qualified study leaders to deliver the service across a broad range of sectors and at all stages of projects and/or programmes.	MoV is embedded across the organization. The value added by the service can be demonstrated qualitatively and quantitatively. MoV is regularly applied at programme or project level.	MoV is embedded in the organization's culture, and the outputs and data derived therefrom are used to contribute to decision-making. There is a programme for and evidence of continual improvement.

- Develop generic value profiles that may be tailored to suit typical subjects that are relevant, together with common areas in which value may be added.
- Develop MoV terminology that is consistent with that used in other processes in the organization to assist its embedding.
- Develop success stories and identify the benefits gained by the use of MoV (internally or by third parties) and disseminate across the organization.
- Develop recording and reporting formats and procedures.
- Allocate explicit roles and responsibilities.
- Introduce a suitable training programme to raise awareness, build culture and assist involvement in MoV studies.

D.6.2 Maintaining the highest level of maturity

Once the organization has achieved the level of maturity to which it aspires, maintaining that level will require discipline and management effort. The principal activities that will be needed will include:

- The implementation of a continuous improvement process, including using lessons learned to inform and refine established processes.
- Maintaining records and undertaking reviews to ensure that MoV is effective in achieving results and supporting decision-making.
- Maintaining training and process improvement.
- Keeping policies and the MoV plan up to date to maintain its relevance.
- Broadening the scope of projects and other activities subject to MoV.
- Continuing efforts to embed and enhance the MoV culture.

D.6.3 Principal benefits

The use of maturity models is increasingly seen as a valuable tool to enhance performance and competitiveness in both public and private sectors. Some of the key benefits that arise include:

- More effective delivery of services and products
- Reduction of wasteful practices through the effective use of MoV
- A higher rate of return on investment
- Greater production efficiency
- Lower production or operational costs due to more efficient processes
- Better-quality outcomes
- Improved customer satisfaction
- Enhanced employee morale
- A means of identifying and implementing management's plans to achieve realistic and achievable goals.

D.6.4 Reasons for use

An organization might choose to use maturity modelling for several different reasons. These could include:

- Assessing the success of introducing and embedding MoV into the organization
- Providing evidence to enhance competitiveness when bidding for providing services to a project

- Understanding strengths and weaknesses better to improve performance
- Assessing the effectiveness of training.

D.7 INDIVIDUAL COMPETENCE MODELS

The foregoing has focused mainly on organizational maturity models. If an organization has elected to develop the means of delivering MoV studies using its own internal resources or if it needs an objective method of assessing the competence of external resource, an individual competence model will be useful.

The primary difference between the organizational maturity model and the individual competence model is that the latter focuses on the individual's ability to undertake complex and strategic MoV studies.

An individual who has qualified in a knowledge-based qualification such as MoV foundation or practitioner level also needs the attributes described in section 7.2, as well as leadership, presentation and facilitation skills, to be fully competent as a study leader.

Various organizations have well-developed training courses to instil the above skills, should potential study leaders not already possess them.

Possession of these skills, together with the knowledge contained in this guide, will enable an individual to deliver formal MoV studies, using the accepted and effective processes described elsewhere in this guide.

Once qualified, the individual can then aspire to improve performance and competence to progress from running simple studies to very complex and strategic studies at programme or project levels.

The competence model below is indicative of the attributes needed by a study leader to achieve the levels indicated. The senior MoV practitioner should develop a suitable competence assessment model tailored to the requirements in his organization.

Assessment of an individual may be undertaken by use of a questionnaire or interview.

Suggested competence levels for each practitioner's understanding and ability to lead a study are:

1 Able to contribute constructively and to help organize an MoV study run by a competent and qualified study leader.

2 Able to plan, arrange and run a simple MoV study, including preparation and submission of reports and agreeing plans for implementing the recommendations.

3 Able to plan, organize and run a series of coordinated studies across one or several projects of medium complexity or to run a single study on a highly complex project. Able to apply qualitative and quantitative value metrics for monetary and non-monetary attributes. Includes responsibility for capturing relevant data in a suitable database for others to use in learning lessons and improving performance. The latter resource may not be available in a smaller organization.

4 Comfortable with leading a team of qualified study leaders and support personnel to conduct MoV at programme level, including consolidating reports prepared by others for reporting to the project board. Sufficiently experienced and qualified to train and mentor others to become MoV study leaders to level 2 competence.

5 Capable of running a programme of MoV activities across the organization, addressing strategic, programme, project and operational levels. Very experienced and able to apply MoV across a broad range of applications and/or disciplines. Qualified to train and mentor others to become MoV study leaders to the highest levels of competence. Contributes to decision-making by senior management.

D.7.1 Progression between levels
An individual at level 1 is unlikely to have had formal accredited training except at foundation level. To progress to level 2 the individual would typically:

- Undergo formal accredited practitioner training including facilitation training
- Have participated in several formal MoV studies led by others
- Led at least two successful formal MoV studies.

Progression from level 2 to higher levels will depend upon the individual acquiring broad experience and practising MoV across a range of subjects of increasing complexity. Such progression will be largely self-motivated and include some or all of the aspects outlined below:

- Demonstrating an eagerness to learn from more experienced study leaders
- Demonstrating an ability to innovate the design of MoV events within the frameworks given in this guide
- Demonstrating the ability to motivate others to contribute actively and constructively in MoV studies
- Preparing and presenting original papers at professional events that advance the acceptance and practice of MoV
- Making positive contributions to embedding MoV in the organization
- Inspiring senior management to commission MoV at increasingly strategic levels
- Adapting practice to learn lessons from previous MoV studies as well as practices adapted from other sectors
- Tailoring MoV processes to suit the organization
- Authoring success stories and case studies and disseminating these across the organization
- Gathering useful qualitative and quantitative data and making it available to others for continuous improvement, and building the culture in the organization.
- Training others to improve their performance.

Glossary

Glossary

abstraction

The level of a function in a hierarchy.

activity

A process, function or task that occurs over time, has recognizable results and is managed. It is usually defined as part of a process or plan.

agile methods

Principally, software development methods that apply the project approach of (often) using short time-boxed iterations where products are incrementally developed. PRINCE2 and MoV are compatible with agile principles.

approval

The formal confirmation that a product is complete and meets its requirements (less any concessions) as defined by its product description.

assumption

A statement that is taken as being true for the purposes of planning, but which could change later. An assumption is made where some facts are not yet known or decided, and is usually reserved for matters of such significance that if they change or turn out not to be true, there will need to be considerable re-planning. These are normally specifically challenged in MoV studies.

attribute

A characteristic or inherent feature.

authority

The right to allocate resources and make decisions (applies to project, stage and team levels).

authorization

The point at which an authority is granted.

baseline

A reference level against which an entity is monitored and controlled.

basic function

The primary purpose of an output, the one function that never changes unless the product or service itself does. If it is not satisfied, the output is worthless. For example, the purpose of a bus stop is to provide a point where people waiting are easily visible to the bus driver, so they can hail the bus. If it doesn't meet this need, it might as well not be built.

benchmark

A product or process against which other products or processes may be compared.

benefit

A measurable improvement resulting from an outcome perceived as an advantage by a stakeholder.

benefits distribution matrix

An illustration of the distribution of benefits against dis-benefits across the organization, i.e. the winners and losers in a change.

benefits management

The identification, definition, tracking, realization and optimization of benefits, usually within a programme which can incorporate benefits identified via an MoV study.

benefits realization

For projects, the practice of aligning the outcome associated with the project with the projected benefits claimed in the business case.

Best Management Practice

A defined and proven method of managing events effectively.

briefing meeting

A meeting at the outset of an MoV activity where the study leader or participants in an MoV activity receive information on the subject under review.

business as usual

Abbreviated to BAU, this is the way the business normally achieves its objectives.

business case

The justification for an organizational activity (strategic, programme, project, operational) which typically contains costs, benefits, risks and timescales and against which continuing viability is tested.

business unit

A discrete component of an organization.

capability

A service, function or operation that enables the organization to exploit opportunities.

change manager

A person who may operate at any level to support benefits realization, focusing on the realization of a particular benefit.

communications plan

A plan of the communication activities that will be established and maintained during the organizational activity (strategic, programme, project, or operational). It typically contains when, what, how and with whom information flows.

competence

The ability of an individual to do something well.

constraints

The restrictions or limitations that a project is bound by. These may be challenged during an MoV study.

contingency

Something that is held in reserve, typically to handle time and cost variances or risks. PRINCE2 does not advocate the use of contingency because estimating variances are managed by setting tolerances; risks are managed through appropriate risk responses (including the fallback response that is contingent on the risk occurring).

cost driver

An activity that results in a cost.

critical path

The line connecting the start of an activity network with the final activity in that network through those activities with zero float; i.e. those activities where any delay will affect the end date of the entire plan. There may be more than one such path. The sum of the activity durations on the critical path will determine the end date of the plan.

critical success factor

An event or measure of activity defining successful delivery by a project, business unit or organization.

cross-cutting

A term used in the public sector to describe issues that affect more than one policy department.

customer

The person or group who commissioned the work and will benefit from the end results.

decision point

A point in the progress of a programme or project at which significant decisions are made.

deliverable

See output.

delivery

The act of implementing a process.

dis-benefit

An outcome perceived as negative by a stakeholder. A dis-benefit is an actual consequence of an activity whereas, by definition, a risk has some uncertainty about whether it will materialize.

earned value analysis

A method for measuring project performance. It indicates how much of the budget should have been spent in view of the amount of work done so far and the task.

embedding

When applied to MoV, it is the consolidation of skills and concepts in a given organization.

end user

The person who uses the final output of a project or delivered service.

esteem value

An attribute of an article or service that is desired for reasons of purely personal interest or preference, or for the social cachet it bestows.

evaluation criteria

A means by which to assess relative value or performance of different options.

exchange value

The value of a particular article or service considered as its worth in exchange for another item, such as gold.

executive

The single individual with overall responsibility for ensuring that a project meets its objectives and delivers the projected benefits. This individual should ensure that the project maintains its business focus, that it has clear authority and that the work, including risks, is actively managed. The executive is the chair of the project board. He or she represents the customer and is responsible for the business case.

expected value

Expected value is calculated by multiplying the average impact by the probability percentage.

expenditure

Consumption of resources.

facilitation

A technique by which a study leader takes a team through a series of processes or techniques in a collaborative manner, resulting in their taking ownership of the outputs.

feasibility study

An early study of a problem to assess whether or not a solution is feasible. The study will normally scope the problem, identify and explore a number of solutions and make a recommendation on what action to take. Part of the work in developing options is to calculate an outline business case for each as one aspect of comparison.

function

What something does, expressed as an active verb and a measurable noun (as closely as possible). It may be tangible (e.g. bears weight) or intangible (e.g. operates intuitively).

function analysis

A method of analysing functions to show appropriate linkages.

Function Analysis Systems Technique

Abbreviated to FAST, this technique uses a hierarchy of functions, expressed in one direction to address 'how' they are delivered, and in another to address 'why'.

function diagram

A diagram expressing a hierarchy of functions.

given

A precondition on the scope of an MoV study, which must be satisfied.

government policy

The translation of a government's political priorities and principles into programmes and courses of action to deliver desired changes.

handover

The transfer of ownership of a set of products to the respective user(s). The set of products is known as a release. There may be more than one handover in the life of a project (phased delivery). The final handover takes place in the Closing a Project process.

hard value analysis

A subset of value engineering for a project that seeks to maximize the value of a physical output. *See* value engineering.

health check

A quality tool that provides a snapshot of the status of a project, programme or portfolio. The purpose of a health check is to gain an objective assessment of how well the project, programme or portfolio is performing relative to its objectives and any relevant processes or standards. A health check differs from a review in that it is a tool used for assurance purposes by the P3O to inform specific actions or capability maturity development plans, whereas a review is part of formal governance arrangements.

ICT

Information and communications technology.

initiation stage

The period from when the project board authorizes initiation to when they authorize the project (or decide not to go ahead with the project). The detailed planning and establishment of the project management infrastructure is covered by the Initiating a Project process.

investment decision

The decision to proceed with a programme or project. Also describes the entire lifecycle of a programme or project from inception (pre-start-up) to use (closure).

issue

A concern, query, request for change, suggestion or off-specification raised during a project. Project issues can be about anything to do with the project.

key performance indicator

Abbreviated to KPI, this is a metric (either financial or non-financial) that is used to set and measure progress towards an organizational objective.

leadership

The ability to direct, influence and motivate others towards a better outcome.

Lean

A management process aimed at eliminating waste in the supply chain.

lower-order function

A function contributing to the delivery of a basic function. These are often important to a successful product or service.

management board

A generic term used to describe either project management boards, programme management boards or portfolio management boards, or any combination based on the P3O context.

management of value

A systematic method to define what value means for organizations, and to communicate it clearly to maximize value across portfolios, programmes, projects and operations.

maturity level

A well-defined evolutionary plateau towards achieving a mature process (five levels are often cited: initial, repeatable, defined, managed and optimizing).

maturity model

A method of assessing organizational capability in a given area of skill.

milestone

A significant event in a plan's schedule, such as completion of key work packages, a technical stage or a management stage.

MoV board

A group of senior managers who advise the MoV senior practitioner on the delivery of the MoV implementation plan.

MoV implementation plan

The plan for delivering the MoV strategy.

MoV programme

A series of interrelated MoV studies across a major project or large organization's service review.

MoV programme plan

The plan for applying MoV to a programme.

MoV progress report

A regular report describing the current progress that has been made in delivering the benefits of a value-improving proposal.

MoV project plan

The plan for applying MoV to a project.

MoV steering group

See MoV board.

MoV study

A combination of activities including preparation, analysis workshop(s), decision building, reporting and implementation.

MoV study handbook

A collation by the study leader of all the information required for successful team participation in an MoV study.

MoV study team

The people who actively contribute to an MoV study.

MoV workshop

A gathering of stakeholders and disciplines relating to a particular study, facilitated to guide participants through the MoV approach.

needs

The benefits that are either essential or desired from the resources applied to a given project.

objective

The intended outcome or goal of a programme, project or organization.

off-project specialist or expert

Someone with knowledge and experience in the subject of the MoV activities who is not involved in the programme project. May be invited to contribute to an MoV study to challenge the MoV study team members and improve the objectivity of their proposals.

OGC Gateway Review

A review of a delivery programme or procurement project carried out at a key decision point by a team of experienced people, independent of the project team.

operations

Business as usual in an organization.

opportunity

An uncertain event that could have a favourable impact on objectives or benefits.

order

The relative level of a function in a hierarchy (higher or lower).

outcome

The result of change, normally affecting real-world behaviour and/or circumstances. Outcomes are desired when a change is conceived. Outcomes are achieved as a result of the activities undertaken to effect the change. In a programme, the outcome is the manifestation of part or all of the new state conceived in the blueprint.

output

A specialist product that is handed over to its user(s). Note that management products are not outputs but are created solely for the purpose of managing the project.

P3M3

The Portfolio, Programme and Project Management Maturity Model that provides a framework with which organizations can assess their current performance and put in place improvement plans.

P3O sponsor

A senior manager with appropriate authority who champions the establishment and evolving operation of the P3O. They will ideally be a member of the main board. See also *Portfolio, Programme and Project Offices*.

Pareto principle

Also known as the '80/20 rule', which states that 80% of gains will come from 20% of study activity.

peer review

Specific reviews of a project or any of its products where personnel from within the organization and/or from other organizations carry out an independent assessment of the project. Peer reviews can be done at any point within a project but are often used at stage-end points.

performance targets

A plan's goals for time, cost, quality, scope, benefits and risk.

PESTLE

Political, economic, social, technological, legal and environment – a technique used generally in organizational change management to undertake an environmental scan at a strategic level.

plan

A detailed proposal for doing or achieving something which specifies the what, when, how and by whom. In PRINCE2 there are only the following types of plan: project plan, stage plan, team plan, exception plan and benefits review plan.

plastic project

A project in which dependencies have been minimized (often by creating a shared platform) so that decisions can be taken at the last responsible moment.

Often used under fast-changing conditions, or where the problem and/or solution spaces are subject to a high degree of uncertainty.

policy

A course of action (or principle) adopted by an organization. A business statement of intent, setting the tone for an organization's culture.

portfolio

The totality of an organization's investment (or segment thereof) in the changes required to achieve its strategic objectives.

Portfolio, Programme and Project Offices

Abbreviated to P3O, this is the decision-enabling and support business model for all business change within an organization. This will include single or multiple physical or virtual structures, e.g. offices (permanent and/or temporary), providing a mix of central and localized functions and services, integration with governance arrangements and the wider business such as other corporate support functions.

post-implementation review

The process of determining the nature and value of benefits achieved and lessons learned from the project. This would need to be repeated at intervals to collate full results.

PPM

An abbreviation for the Portfolio, Programme and Project Management series of guides aimed at improving the performance of those involved in portfolio, programme and project management. PPM is the accepted term in the industry and covers portfolio as well as programme and project management issues.

practitioner

Someone who is competent in and regularly leads MoV activities.

primary function

A function with a close and direct link to the study objectives. *See also* value driver.

procedure

A series of actions for a particular aspect of project management established specifically for the project – for example, a risk management procedure.

process

A structured set of activities designed to accomplish a specific objective. A process takes one or more defined inputs and turns them into defined outputs.

product

An input or output, whether tangible or intangible, that can be described in advance, created and tested.

programme

A temporary flexible organization structure created to coordinate, direct and oversee the implementation of a set of related projects and activities in order to deliver outcomes and benefits related to the organization's strategic objectives. A programme is likely to have a life that spans several years.

programme board

A group that supports the senior responsible owner to deliver the programme.

programme management

The coordinated organization, direction and implementation of a dossier of projects and activities that together achieve outcomes and realize benefits that are of strategic importance.

programme manager

The role responsible for the set-up, management and delivery of the programme, typically allocated to a single individual.

programme office

The function providing the information hub for the programme and its delivery objectives; could provide support for more than one programme.

project

A temporary organization that is created for the purpose of delivering one or more business products according to an agreed business case.

project brief

A statement that describes the purpose and cost, time and performance requirements and constraints for a project. It is created pre-project during the Starting up a Project process and is used during the Initiating a Project process to create the Project Initiation Documentation and its components. It is superseded by the Project Initiation Documentation and not maintained.

project control tool

A process or technique for informing management to enable them to maintain control over the progress of a project.

project lifecycle

The period from the start up of a project to the acceptance of the project product.

project management

The planning, delegating, monitoring and control of all aspects of the project, and the motivation of those involved, to achieve the project objectives within the expected performance targets for time, cost, quality, scope, benefits and risks.

project management team

The entire management structure of the project board, and project manager, plus any team manager, project assurance and project support roles.

project management team structure

An organization chart showing the people assigned to the project management team roles to be used and their delegation and reporting relationships.

project manager or executive

The person with authority and responsibility to manage a project on a day–to-day basis to deliver the required products within the constraints agreed by the project board.

project office

A temporary office set up to support the delivery of a specific change initiative being delivered as a project. If used, the project office undertakes the responsibility of the project support role.

project sponsor

The main driving force behind a project.

project start-up notification

Advice to the host location that the project is about to start and requesting any required project support services.

project support

An administrative role in the project management team. Project support can be in the form of advice and help with project management tools, guidance, administrative services such as filing, and the collection of actual data.

project support office

A group set up to provide certain administrative services to the project manager. Often the group provides its services to many projects in parallel.

proposal implementation plan

A plan for implementing value-improving proposals to realize their expected benefits.

proposal owner

The individual responsible for developing a value-improving proposals.

public sector

Activities undertaken without a profit motive for the greater good and/or for which specific usage cannot be monitored (e.g. street lighting), paid for by the public at large via taxation.

records

Dynamic management products that maintain information regarding project progress.

requirements

A description of the user's needs.

risk

An uncertain event or set of events which, should it occur, will have an effect on the achievement of objectives. A risk is measured by a combination of the probability of a perceived threat or opportunity occurring and the magnitude of its impact on objectives.

risk management

The systematic application of principles, approach and processes to the tasks of identifying and assessing risks, and then planning and implementing risk responses.

scenario

A package of value-improving proposals.

schedule

A graphical representation of a plan (for example, a Gantt chart), typically describing a sequence of tasks, together with resource allocations, which collectively deliver the plan.

scope

For a plan, the sum total of its products and the extent of their requirements. It is described by the product breakdown structure for the plan and associated product descriptions.

senior management

Top management responsible for embedding or running MoV activities.

senior MoV practitioner

The individual charged with leading the implementation of the MoV implementation plan.

senior responsible owner

Abbreviated to SRO, this is a UK government term for the individual responsible for ensuring that a project or programme of change meets its objectives and delivers the projected benefits. The person should be the owner of the overall business change that is being supported by the project. The senior responsible owner should ensure that the change maintains its business focus, that it has clear authority, and that the context, including risks, is actively managed. This individual must be senior and must take personal responsibility for successful delivery of the project. The SRO should be recognized as the owner throughout the organization. The SRO appoints the project's executive (or in some cases may elect to be the executive).

sensitivity analysis

A technique for testing the robustness of a calculation or model by assessing the impact of varying the input, to reflect the risk that the calculation or model might not be accurate.

Six Sigma

A management process aimed at minimizing defects and increasing efficiency.

soft value analysis

A subset of value analysis for a project that seeks to maximize value of an intangible output. Commonly associated with service delivery. See value analysis.

soft value management

MoV aimed at messy, strategic and conceptual decision-making, with an emphasis on integrated outcomes from projects (rather than merely coordinated) and a need for wider involvement.

specification

A detailed statement of what the user wants in terms of products, what these should look like, what they should do and with what they should interface.

sponsor

The main driving force behind a programme or project.

stakeholder

Any individual, group or organization that can affect, be affected by, or perceive itself to be affected by an initiative (programme, project, activity, risk).

stakeholder analysis

A method of assessing the impact of a study on people's concerns and attitudes with regard to a given issue and their influence on its outcome.

stakeholder map

A diagram, table or matrix showing stakeholders and their particular interests in the programme.

start up

The pre-project activities undertaken by the executive and the project manager to produce the outline business case, project brief and initiation stage plan.

strategy

An approach or line to take, designed to achieve a long-term aim. Strategies can exist at all levels – portfolio, programme and project.

study definition

Clear articulation of objectives.

study leader

A qualified practitioner who organizes and/or facilitates an MoV study or programme of studies. This term is also used of the individual responsible for planning and conducting a study.

study leader's handbook

Guidance for study leaders prepared by the senior MoV practitioner.

subject

The process or product under review during MoV activities.

support office

A formal or informal group of people who can provide services to support the implementation of MoV within the organization in its application to projects.

tailoring

The appropriate use of PRINCE2 on any given project, ensuring that there is the correct amount of planning, control, governance and use of the processes and themes (whereas the adoption of PRINCE2 across an organization is known as 'embedding').

team leader

The person appointed from time to time by the senior MoV practitioner to be responsible for leading and managing a group of people through a process to deliver an output, e.g. a health check.

technique

A procedure used to accomplish a specific activity or task.

third sector

The not-for-profit organizations outside the public sector. These include volunteer organizations and charities.

trade-off

In the context of MoV, transferring from one attribute to another to add more value.

user

The person or group who will use one or more of the project's products.

utility value

The utility value of an item is the primary requirement that an individual has of that item, which must be addressed for the item to have any worth.

value

The benefits delivered in proportion to the resources put into acquiring them.

value analysis

A method of analysing value (see also value engineering) within a product, building or process. Commonly abbreviated to VA.

value driver

A function that must be delivered to contribute to the project objectives. Value drivers must, in aggregate, be necessary and sufficient to achieve the project objectives in full. A primary value driver is equivalent to a primary function.

value engineering

A method of maximizing value (see also value analysis) within a design. Commonly abbreviated to VE.

value for money ratio

The ratio of benefits, monetary or non-monetary, to investment made or resources committed. A measure of value for money.

value-improving proposal

A statement setting out a description of a proposed improvement, the advantages and disadvantages of implementation and its impact on cost, time and performance.

value index

A measure of how well an option, project or product satisfies an individual value driver or the aggregate of all value drivers. It represents a measure of customer satisfaction.

value management

Widely used term that is synonymous with management of value (MoV). A systematic method to define what value means for organizations, and to communicate it clearly to maximize value across portfolios, programmes, projects and operations.

value metrics

Attributes used for measuring performance against value drivers.

value profile

A representation of the relative importance of the primary value drivers to the client body and end users.

value ratio

The ratio between benefits, monetary or non-monetary, and expenditure of resources. A measure of value.

value score

The product of the performance of an option or proposal, assessed on a scale of 1–10, and the weighting of a value driver against which it is being assessed.

value tree

A diagram that shows the relationship between, and the hierarchy of, value drivers.

version

A specific baseline of a product. Versions typically use naming conventions that enable the sequence or date of the baseline to be identified. For example, project plan version 2 is the baseline after project plan version 1.

waterfall method

A development approach that is linear and sequential with distinct goals for each phase of development. Once a phase of development is completed, the development proceeds to the next phase and earlier phases are not revisited (hence the analogy that water flowing down a mountain cannot go back).

weighting

A method of prioritizing attributes or functions.

Index

Index